The Art of Communicating

Also by Thich Nhat Hanh

The Art of Communicating

Thich Nhat Hanh

HarperOne
An Imprint of HarperCollins*Publishers*

HarperOne

HarperCollins books may be purchased for educational, business, or sales promotional use. For information, please e-mail the Special Markets Department at SPsales@harpercollins.com.

HarperCollins website: http://www.harpercollins.com

HarperCollins®, ▣®, and HarperOne™ are
trademarks of HarperCollins Publishers.

FIRST EDITION

Library of Congress Cataloging-in-Publication Data

Nhat Hanh, Thich.
The art of communicating / Thich Nhat Hanh. — First edition.
pages cm
ISBN 978–0–06–222467–5
1. Interpersonal communication—Religious aspects. 2. Interpersonal relations—Religious aspects. 3. Religious life—Buddhism. I. Title.
BL629.5.C67N43   2013
294.3'444—dc23   2013016427

13 14 15 16 17 RRD(H) 10 9 8 7 6 5 4 3 2 1

Contents

1

Essential Food

Nothing can survive without food. Everything we consume acts either to heal us or to poison us. We tend to think of nourishment only as what we take in through our mouths, but what we consume with our eyes, our ears, our noses, our tongues, and our bodies is also food. The conversations going on around us, and those we participate in, are also food. Are we consuming and creating the kind of food that is healthy for us and helps us grow?

When we say something that nourishes us and uplifts the people around us, we are feeding love and compassion. When we speak and act in a way that causes tension and anger, we are nourishing violence and suffering.

We often ingest toxic communication from those around us and from what we watch and read. Are we ingesting things that grow our understanding and compassion? If so, that's good food. Often, we ingest communication that makes us feel bad or insecure about ourselves or judgmental and superior to others. We can think about our communication in terms of nourishment and consumption. The Internet is an item of consumption, full of nutrients that are both healing and toxic. It's so easy to ingest a lot in just a few minutes online. This doesn't mean you shouldn't use the Internet, but you should be conscious of what you are reading and watching.

When you work with your computer for three or four hours, you are totally lost. It's like eating french fries. You shouldn't eat french fries all day, and you shouldn't be on the computer all day. A few french fries, a few hours, are probably all most of us need.

What you read and write can help you heal, so be thoughtful about what you consume. When you write an e-mail or a letter that is full of understanding and compassion, you are nourishing yourself during the time you write that letter. Even if it's just a short note, everything you're writing down can nourish you and the person to whom you are writing.

Consuming with Mindfulness

How can you tell what communication is healthy and what is toxic? The energy of mindfulness is a necessary ingredient in healthy communication. Mindfulness requires letting go of judgment, returning to an awareness of the breath and the body, and bringing your full attention to what is in you and around you. This helps you notice whether the thought you just produced is healthy or unhealthy, compassionate or unkind.

Conversation is a source of nourishment. We all get lonely and want to talk with someone. But when you have a conversation with another person, what that person says may be full of toxins, like hate, anger, and frustration. When you listen to what others say, you're consuming those toxins. You're bringing toxins into your consciousness and your body. That's why mindfulness of speaking and mindfulness of listening are very important.

Toxic conversation can be difficult to avoid, especially at work. If it is going on around you, be aware. You need to have enough mindful awareness not to absorb these kinds of suffering. You have to protect yourself with the energy of compassion so that when you listen, instead of consuming toxins, you're actively producing more compassion in yourself. When you listen in this way, compassion protects you and the other person suffers less.

You absorb the thoughts, speech, and actions you produce and those contained in the communications of those around you. That is a form of consumption. So

5

when you read something, when you listen to someone, you should be careful not to allow the toxins to ruin your health and bring suffering to you and to the other person or group of people.

To illustrate this truth, the Buddha used the graphic image of a cow that has a skin disease. The cow is attacked by all kinds of insects and microorganisms coming from the soil, coming from the trees, coming from the water. Without skin, a cow can't protect herself. Mindfulness is our skin. Without mindfulness, we may take in things that are toxic to our body and mind.

Even when you simply drive your car through the city, you consume. The advertisements hit your eyes, and you're forced to consume them. You hear sounds; you may even say things that are the products of too much toxic consumption. We have to protect ourselves with mindful consumption. Mindful communication is part of this. We can communicate in such a way as to solidify the peace and compassion in ourselves and bring joy to others.

Relationships Don't Survive Without the Right Food

Many of us suffer because of difficult communication. We feel misunderstood, especially by those we love. In a relationship, we are nourishment for each other. So we have to select the kind of food we offer the other person, the kind of food that can help our relationships thrive. Everything—including love, hate, and suffering—needs food to continue. If suffering continues, it's because we keep feeding our suffering. Every time we speak without mindful awareness, we are feeding our suffering.

With mindful awareness, we can look into the nature of our suffering and find out what kind of food we have been supplying to keep it alive. When we find the source of nourishment for our suffering, we can cut off that supply, and our suffering will fade.

Often a romantic relationship begins beautifully, but then, because we don't know how to nourish our love, the relationship begins to die. Communication can bring it back to life. Every thought you produce in your head, in your heart—in China they say, "in your belly"—feeds that relationship. When you produce a thought that carries suspicion, anger, fear, irritation, that thought is not nourishing to you or to the other person. If the relationship has become difficult, it's because we've nourished our judgment and our anger, and we haven't nourished our compassion.

One day in Plum Village, the French retreat center where I live, I gave a talk about how we needed to nourish our loved ones by practicing loving communication. I spoke about our relationships as flowers that need watering with love and communication to grow. There was a woman sitting near the front who was crying the whole time.

After the talk, I went to her husband, and I said, "My dear friend, your flower needs some watering." Her husband had been at the talk and knew about loving speech, but sometimes we all need a friend to remind us. So, after lunch, the man took his wife for a drive in the country. They just had an hour or so but he focused on watering the good seeds the whole drive.

When they came back, she seemed completely transformed, very happy and joyful. Their children were very surprised, because in the morning when their parents had left, they'd been sad and irritable. So in just an hour, you can transform another person and yourself, just with the practice of watering the good seeds. This is applied mindfulness in action; it's not theoretical.

Nourishing and healing communication is the food of our relationships. Sometimes one cruel utterance can make the other person suffer for many years, and we will suffer for many years too. In a state of anger or fear, we may say something that can be poisonous and destructive. If we swallow poison, it can stay within us for a long time, slowly killing our relationship. We may not even know what we said or did that started to poison the relationship. But we have the antidote: mindful compassion and loving communication. Love, respect, and friendship all need food to survive. With mindfulness we can produce thoughts, speech, and actions that will feed our relationships and help them grow and thrive.

2

Communicating
with Yourself

Loneliness is the suffering of our time. Even if we're surrounded by others, we can feel very alone. We are lonely together. There's a vacuum inside us. It makes us feel uncomfortable, so we try to fill it up by connecting with other people. We believe that if we're able to connect, the feeling of loneliness will disappear.

Technology supplies us with many devices to help us stay connected. But even when we're connected, we continue to feel lonely. We check our e-mail, send text messages, and post updates several times a day. We want to share and receive. We might spend our whole day connecting but not reduce the loneliness we feel.

We all hunger for love, but we don't know how to generate love in order to feed ourselves with it. When we're empty, we use technology to try to dissipate the feeling of loneliness, but it doesn't work. We have the Internet, e-mail, video conferencing, texting and posting, apps, letters, and cell phones. We have everything. And yet it's not at all certain that we have improved our communication.

Many of us have cell phones. We want to be in touch with other people. But we shouldn't put too much faith in our phones. I don't have one, but I don't feel out of touch with the world. In fact, without a mobile device, I have more time for myself and for others. You believe that having your phone helps you to communicate. But if the content of your speech is not authentic, talking or texting on a device doesn't mean you're communicating with another person.

We believe too much in the technologies of communication. Behind all these instruments we have the mind, the most fundamental instrument for communication. If our minds are blocked, there is no device that will make up for our inability to communicate with ourselves or others.

Connecting Internally

Many of us spend a lot of time in meetings or e-mailing with others, and not a lot of time communicating with ourselves. The result is that we don't know what is going on within us. It may be a mess inside. How, then, can we communicate with another person?

We think that with all our technological devices we can connect, but this is an illusion. In daily life we're disconnected from ourselves. We walk, but we don't know that we're walking. We're here, but we don't know that we're here. We're alive, but we don't know that we're alive. Throughout the day, we lose ourselves.

To stop and communicate with yourself is a revolutionary act. You sit down and stop that state of being lost, of not being yourself. You begin by just stopping whatever you're doing, sitting down, and connecting with yourself. This is called mindful awareness. Mindfulness is full awareness of the present moment. You don't need an iPhone or a computer. You just need to sit down and breathe in and out. In just a few seconds, you can connect with yourself. You know what is going on in your body, your feelings, your emotions, and your perceptions.

Digital Purpose

When you don't feel you can communicate well in person or wonder if what you say will be hard for the other person to hear, sometimes the best way to communicate is to write a letter or an e-mail. If you can write a letter that's full of understanding and compassion, then during the time of writing that letter you will nourish yourself. Everything you write will be nourishing for the person you are writing to, and first of all for you. The other person hasn't received the e-mail or letter yet, but while typing the letter you are nourishing yourself, because what you're saying in the letter is full of compassion and understanding.

Especially at the beginning of your practice, it may be easier for you to practice mindful communication in writing. Writing this way is good for our health. We can send an e-mail, we can text, and we can talk on the phone and use mindful communication. If our message is full of understanding and compassion, we'll be able to remove fear and anger from the other person. So next time you hold the phone, look at it and remember that its purpose is to help you communicate with compassion.

Usually, we are in a hurry to send our e-mails and texts. As soon as we finish writing them, we press send and they are gone. But there's no need to rush. We always have time for at least one in-breath and out-breath before we pick up the phone or before we press send on a text or e-mail. If we do this, there is a much greater chance that we will be putting more compassion-ate communication out into the world.

Coming Home

When we begin to practice mindful awareness, we start the path home to ourselves. Home is the place where loneli-ness disappears. When we're home, we feel warm, comfort-able, safe, fulfilled. We've gone away from our homes for a long time, and our homes have become neglected.

But the path back home is not long. Home is inside us. Going home requires only sitting down and being with yourself, accepting the situation as it is. Yes, it might be a mess in there, but we accept it because we know we have left home for a long time. So now we're home. With our in-breath and our out-breath, our mindful breathing, we begin to tidy up our homes.

Communicating with the Breath

The path home begins with your breath. If you know how to breathe, you can learn how to walk, how to sit, how to eat your meal, and how to work in mindfulness so that you can begin to know yourself. When you breathe in, you come back to yourself. When you breathe out, you release any tension. Once you can communicate with yourself, you'll be able to communicate outwardly with more clarity. The way in is the way out.

Mindful breathing is a means of communication, just like a phone. It promotes communication between the mind and the body. It helps us know what we're feeling. We're breathing all the time, but we rarely pay attention to our breath, unless our breathing is uncomfortable or restricted.

With mindful breathing, when we breathe in we know we're breathing in. When we breathe out we know we're breathing out. When we breathe in, we bring our attention to our in-breath. To remind ourselves to pay attention to our breath, we can say silently:

Breathing in, I know I'm breathing in.
Breathing out, I know I'm breathing out.

"The air is entering my body. The air is leaving my body." Follow your in-breath and out-breath all the way through. Suppose your in-breath lasts four seconds. During the time of breathing in, allow your attention to rest entirely on your in-breath, without interruption. During the time of breathing out, focus entirely on your out-breath. You are with your in-breath and your out-breath. You are not with anything else. You are your in-breath and your out-breath.

Breathing in and breathing out is a practice of freedom. When we focus our attention on our breath, we release everything else, including worries or fears about the future and regrets or sorrows about the past. Focusing on the breath, we notice what we're feeling in the present moment. We can do this throughout the day, enjoying the twenty-four hours that have been given us to breathe in and out. We can be there for ourselves. It takes only a few seconds to breathe in and set yourself free.

We know when others are breathing in and out mindfully; we can see it when we look at them. They look free. If we're overloaded with fear, anger, regret, or anxiety, we're not free, no matter what position we hold in society or how much money we have. Real freedom only comes when we're able to release our suffering and come home. Freedom is the most precious thing there is. It is the foundation of happiness, and it is available to us with each conscious breath.

Nonthinking and Nontalking

Happiness is possible when you're in communication with yourself. To do this, you have to leave your telephone behind. When you attend a meeting or an event, you turn off your telephone. Why? Because you want to communicate and absorb others' communication. It is the same when communicating with yourself. This kind of communication is not possible with the phone. We're used to thinking a lot and talking a lot. But to communicate with ourselves, we need to practice nonthinking and nontalking.

Nonthinking is a very important practice. Of course, thinking and talking can be productive too, especially when our minds and feelings are clear. But a lot of our thinking is caught up in dwelling on the past, trying to control the future, generating misperceptions, and worrying about what others are thinking.

A misperception can happen in a moment, in a flash. As soon as we have a perception, we're caught by it. So anything we say or do based on that perception can be dangerous. It's better not to say or do anything! That's why in the Zen tradition they say the paths of talking and of thinking should be cut off. The path of speech is cut off because if you continue to talk, you continue to be caught in your words.

Mindful breathing is a practice of nonthinking and nontalking. Without thinking and talking, there is no obstacle to get in the way of our enjoyment of the present moment. It's enjoyable to breathe in, to breathe out; it's enjoyable to sit, to walk, to eat breakfast, to take a shower, to clean the bathroom, to work in the vegetable garden. When we stop talking and thinking and we listen mindfully to ourselves, one thing we will notice is our greater capacity and opportunities for joy.

The other thing that happens when we stop thinking and talking and we begin listening to ourselves is that we notice the suffering present in our lives. There may be tension and pain in our bodies. We may have old pains and fears or new pains and fears, which we have hidden under our talking and texting and thinking.

Mindfulness lets us listen to the pain, the sorrow, and the fear inside. When we see that some suffering or some pain is coming up, we don't try to run away from it. In fact, we have to go back and take care of it. We're not afraid of being overwhelmed, because we know how to breathe and how to walk so as to generate enough energy of mindfulness to recognize and take care of the suffering. If you have enough mindfulness generated by the practice of mindful breathing and walking, you're no longer afraid to be with yourself.

If I am free of needing a mobile phone, it's because I

carry mindfulness with me, like a guardian angel on my shoulder. The angel is always with me when I practice. It helps me be unafraid of whatever suffering or pain arises. It's much more important to keep your mindfulness with you than to keep your mobile phone. You think that you're safe when carrying your phone. But the truth is that mindfulness will do much more than a phone to protect you, to help you suffer less, and to improve your communication.

Come Back

The quiet of nonthinking and nontalking gives us the space to truly listen to ourselves. We don't have to try to get away from our suffering. We don't have to cover up what is unpleasant in us. In fact, we try to be there for ourselves, to understand, so that we can transform.

Please do come back home and listen. If you don't communicate well with yourself, you cannot communicate well with another person. Come back again and again and communicate lovingly with yourself. That is the practice. You have to go back to yourself and listen to the happiness you may have in this moment; listen to the suffering in your body and in your mind, and learn how to embrace it and bring relief.

Communicating with the Body

As long as we have mindfulness with us, we can breathe mindfully throughout the day as we go about our daily activities. But our mindfulness will be stronger and we'll get more healing and communicate more successfully if we take the time to pause and sit quietly for a few moments. When a newly freed Nelson Mandela came to France for a visit, a journalist asked him what he would most like to do. He said, "Sit down and do nothing." Since his release from prison and his official entry into politics, he hadn't had any time to just enjoy sitting. We should make time to sit, even if it's for only a few minutes a day, because sitting is a pleasure.

Whenever we're restless and don't know what to do, that is a good time to sit down. It's good to sit when we're peaceful too, as a way of nurturing a habit and practice of sitting. When we stop and sit, we can begin right away to follow our in-breath and out-breath. Immediately, we can enjoy breathing in and breathing out, and everything gets a little bit better because the present moment becomes available to us.

Breathe in a way that gives you pleasure. When you sit and breathe mindfully, your mind and body finally get to communicate and come together. This is a kind of miracle because usually the mind is in one place and the body in another. The mind is caught in the details of your projects to be done today, your sorrow about the past, or your anxiety about the future. Your mind isn't anywhere near your body.

When you breathe in mindfully, there is a happy reunion between body and mind. This doesn't take any fancy technique. Just by sitting and breathing mindfully, you're bringing your mind home to your body. Your body is an essential part of your home. When you spend many hours with your computer, you may forget entirely that you have a body until it's too achy, stiff, or tense for you to ignore. You need to take breaks and return to your body before it gets to that point.

To bring more awareness to the connection between body and mind, you can say to yourself:

Breathing in, I'm aware of my body.
Breathing out, I release all the tension in my body.

Take Yourself for a Walk

Mindful walking is a wonderful way to bring together body and mind. It also allows you the additional opportunity to communicate with something outside yourself that is nourishing and healing: the earth. When you take a step with full awareness that you are taking a step on the ground and the earth, there is no distinction between body and mind. Your body is your breathing. Your body is your feet. Your body is your lungs. And when you are connected with body, feet, breath, and lungs, you are home.

Every step brings you home to the here and the now, so you can connect with yourself, your body, and your feelings. That is a real connection. You don't need a device that tells you how many friends you have or how many steps you've walked or how many calories you've burned.

When you walk mindfully, integrate your breath with each step and focus on your foot connecting with the ground. You're aware that you're making a step, and you stop thinking altogether. When you think, you get lost in your thinking. You don't know what's going on in your body, in your feelings, or in the world. If you think while you walk, you're not really walking.

Instead, focus your attention on your breath and your step. Be aware of your foot, its movement, and the ground you're touching. While you focus your attention on making the step, you are free, because in that time your mind is only with the step you are making. Your mind is no longer carried off into the future or the past. You take one step, and you are free.

While you walk, you can say to yourself, *I have arrived. I am home.* These words are not a mere declaration or an affirmation practice. They are a realization. You don't need to run anywhere. Many of us have run all our lives. Now we get to live life properly.

Home is the here and the now, where all the wonders of life are already available, where the wonder that is your body is available. You can't arrive fully in the here and the now unless you invest your whole body and mind into the present moment. If you haven't arrived one hundred percent, stop where you are and don't take another step. Stay there and breathe until you're sure you have arrived one hundred percent. Then you can smile a smile of victory. It's probably best to do that only when you are enjoying mindful walking alone; if you are around other people, you may create a traffic jam.

You don't need an app or an outsider to tell you whether you have arrived. You will know you have arrived because you will recognize that you're comfortable being. When you walk from the parking lot to your office, go home in each step. Recover yourself and connect with yourself during every step. No matter where you're going, you can walk as a free person on this planet Earth and enjoy every step.

Walking on the Earth Heals Our Alienation

Many of us live in a way that alienates us from the earth and from our own bodies. Most of us live very isolated from each other. We humans can get extremely lonely. We're separated not just from the earth and from each other but from our own selves. We spend many hours every day forgetting we have bodies. But if we begin to practice breathing mindfully and listening to the body, we can also begin to look deeply and see that the earth is all around us. We touch the earth, and we are no longer alienated from our own bodies or from the body of the earth.

We commonly think of the earth as our "environment," but looking more deeply, we see that the earth is a wonderful living reality. Often, when we feel alone, we forget that we can connect directly with the earth. When we bring mindfulness to our steps, these steps can bring us back in touch with our own bodies and with the body of the earth. These steps can rescue us from our alienation.

Connecting to Our Suffering

When we begin to breathe mindfully and listen to our bodies, we become aware of feelings of suffering that we've been ignoring. We hold these feelings in our bodies as well as our minds. Our suffering has been trying to communicate with us, to let us know it is there, but we have spent a lot of time and energy ignoring it.

When we begin breathing mindfully, feelings of loneliness, sadness, fear, and anxiety may come up. When that happens, we don't need to do anything right away. We can just continue to follow our in-breath and our out-breath. We don't tell our fear to go away; we recognize it. We don't tell our anger to go away; we acknowledge it. These feelings are like a small child tugging at our sleeves. Pick them up and hold them tenderly. Acknowledging our feelings without judging them or pushing them away, embracing them with mindfulness, is an act of homecoming.

The Suffering of Our Ancestors

We know that the suffering inside us contains the suffering of our fathers, our mothers, and our ancestors. Our ancestors may not have had a chance to get in touch with the practice of mindfulness, which could help them transform their suffering. That is why they have transmitted their unresolved suffering to us. If we are able to understand that suffering and thereby transform it, we are healing our parents and our ancestors as well as ourselves.

Our suffering reflects the suffering of the world. Discrimination, exploitation, poverty, and fear cause a lot of suffering in those around us. Our suffering also reflects the suffering of others. We may be motivated by the desire to do something to help relieve the suffering in the world. How can we do that without understanding the nature of suffering? If we understand our own suffering, it will become much easier for us to understand the suffering of others and of the world. We may have the intention to do something or be someone that can help the world suffer less, but unless we can listen to and acknowledge our own suffering, we will not really be able to help.

Listening Deeply

The amount of suffering inside us and around us can be overwhelming. Usually we don't like to be in touch with it because we believe it's unpleasant. The marketplace provides us with everything imaginable to help us run away from ourselves. We consume all these products in order to ignore and cover up the suffering in us. Even if we're not hungry, we eat. When we watch television, even if the program isn't very good, we don't have the courage to turn it off, because we know that when we turn it off we may have to go back to ourselves and get in touch with the suffering inside. We consume not because we need to consume but because we're afraid of encountering the suffering inside us.

But there is a way of getting in touch with the suffering without being overwhelmed by it. We try to avoid suffering, but suffering is useful. We *need* suffering. Going back to listen and understand our suffering brings about the birth of compassion and love. If we take the time to listen deeply to our own suffering, we will be able to understand it. Any suffering that has not been released and reconciled will continue. Until it has been understood and transformed, we carry with us not just our own suffering but also that of our parents and our ancestors. Getting in touch with the suffering that has been passed down to us helps us understand our own suffering. Understanding suffering gives rise to compassion. Love is born, and right away we suffer less. If we understand the nature and the roots of our suffering, the path leading to the cessation of the suffering will appear in front of us. Knowing there is a way out, a path, brings us relief, and we no longer need to be afraid.

Suffering Brings Happiness

Understanding suffering always brings compassion. If we don't understand suffering, we don't understand happiness. If we know how to take good care of suffering, we will know how to take good care of happiness. We need suffering to grow happiness. The fact is that suffering and happiness always go together. When we understand suffering, we will understand happiness. If we know how to handle suffering, we will know how to handle happiness and produce happiness.

If a lotus is to grow, it needs to be rooted in the mud. Compassion is born from understanding suffering. We all should learn to embrace our own suffering, to listen to it deeply, and to have a deep look into its nature. In doing so, we allow the energy of love and compassion to be born. When the energy of compassion is born, right away we suffer less. When we suffer less, when we have compassion for ourselves, we can more easily understand the suffering of another person and of the world. Then our communication with others will be based on the desire to understand rather than the desire to prove ourselves right or make ourselves feel better. We will have only the intention to help.

Understanding Our Own Suffering
Helps Us Understand Others

I know a woman from Washington, D.C., who at one time planned to commit suicide because she couldn't see any way out of the suffering she was feeling. She had no hope. She had a very difficult relationship with her husband, and also with their three children. She had a friend who wanted her to listen to one of my talks on deep listening and loving speech. She refused because she was Catholic and she thought that listening to a Buddhist teaching meant she wasn't being true to her faith.

On the night she planned to kill herself, she telephoned her friend to say good-bye. Her friend said, "Before you kill yourself, come say good-bye to me. Take a taxi." She came, and when she got there, her friend asked her, as a favor, to listen to the tape before she killed herself. Reluctantly she said, "All right, before dying I'll satisfy your wish."

After listening to the tape, she was curious and decided to go to a mindfulness retreat. At the retreat, she began to really listen to her own suffering. Before that, she had thought the only way to end her suffering was to kill herself. It was too painful to listen. But she learned how to stay with her breath so she could be with her suffering.

She found that she had created a lot of wrong perceptions and had nurtured a lot of anger. She had thought that her husband and her family had created all her suffering, but now she saw that she was co-responsible for her suffering. She had thought that her husband didn't suffer, that he just made her suffer. But now her understanding was quite different, and she was able to see the suffering in her husband. This was quite an achievement. When you see the suffering inside yourself, you can see the suffering in the other person, and you can see your part, your responsibility, in creating the suffering in yourself and in the other person.

The night when she came back from the retreat, she came and sat close to her husband. This was something very new, coming and sitting near him. She sat for a long time, and then she began to talk. She said, "I know you have suffered so much during the past many years. I couldn't help you. I made the situation worse. It wasn't my intention to make you suffer. It was just because I didn't understand you. I didn't see the suffering inside you. Tell me about your difficulties. Please help me understand." She was able to use this kind of loving speech. Her husband began to cry like a baby, because for so many years she hadn't talked to him in a loving way. Their relationship had been very beautiful in the beginning. But it had become filled with resentment and arguments and lacked any real communication. That night began their journey to reconciliation. Two weeks later, the couple came with their children to tell me this story.

Loving Yourself Is the Basis for Compassion

We tend to think we already know and understand our loved ones very well, but that may not be so. If we haven't understood our own suffering and our own perceptions, how can we understand the suffering of another person? We shouldn't be too sure that we understand everything about the other person. We have to ask, "Do I understand myself enough? Do I understand my suffering and its roots?"

Once you have some understanding and insight into your own suffering, you begin to be better at understanding and communicating with someone else. If you can't accept yourself—if you hate yourself and get angry with yourself—how can you love another person and communicate love to him or her?

Self-understanding is crucial for understanding another person; self-love is crucial for loving others. When you've understood your suffering, you suffer less, and you are capable of understanding another person's suffering much more easily. When you can recognize the suffering in the other person and see how that suffering came about, compassion arises. You no longer have the desire to punish or blame the other person. You can listen deeply, and when you speak there is compassion and understanding in your speech. The person with whom you're speaking will feel much more comfortable, because there is understanding and love in your voice.

Coming home to ourselves to understand our suffering and its roots is the first step. Once we understand our suffering and how it came about, we're in a position to communicate with others in such a way that they also suffer less. Our relationships depend on the capacity of each of us to understand our own difficulties and aspirations and those of others.

When you can truly come home to yourself and listen to yourself, you can profit from every moment given you to live. You can enjoy every moment. With good internal communication facilitated by mindful breathing, you can begin to understand yourself, understand your suffering, and understand your happiness. Knowing how to handle suffering, you know at the same time how to produce happiness. And if you're truly happy, we all profit from your happiness. We need happy people in this world.

3

The Keys to
Communicating with Others

As you connect with yourself, you begin connecting more deeply with other people. Without the first step, the second step isn't possible. Don't neglect to reserve some time alone each day for communicating with yourself.

All of us still have misperceptions and suffering. When we communicate with others, we should be aware that the suffering we have yet to heal and our perceptions are also there. If we can be aware of our in-breath and out-breath, we will remember that the one goal of compassionate communication is to help others suffer less. If we remember this, we've already succeeded. We're already contributing to more joy and less suffering.

Saying Hello

It's helpful to remember at the beginning of every communication with another person that there is a Buddha inside each of us. "The Buddha" is just a name for the most understanding and compassionate person it's possible to be. You may call it something else if you wish, like wisdom or God. We can breathe, smile, and walk in such a way that this person in us has a chance to manifest.

Where I live in Plum Village, every time you meet someone on your way somewhere, you join your palms and bow to him or to her with respect, because you know that there is a Buddha inside that person. Even if that person isn't looking or acting like a Buddha, the capacity for love and compassion is in him or her. If you know how to bow with respect and freshness, you can help the Buddha in him or her to come out. To join your palms and bow like this isn't mere ritual. It's a practice of awakening.

While you bring your hands up and put your palms together, breathe in and out mindfully. Your two hands form a flower, a lotus bud. If you do this with genuine intention, you will likely be able to see the possibilities in the other person. As you breathe, you may want to say silently:

A lotus for you.
A Buddha to be.

When you join your palms, there should be concentration in you so you're not just going through the motions. The lotus flower of your hands is an offering to the person in front of you. When you bow, you recognize the beauty in the other person.

In many Asian countries, when we meet each other we don't shake hands like in the West. We just join our palms and bow. About 160 years ago, the French came to Vietnam, and they taught us how to shake hands. In the beginning we thought it was funny to shake hands like that, but we learned quite quickly. Now everyone knows how to shake hands, but we still like to join our palms and bow, especially in the temple. It may not be appropriate in your life or workplace for you to join your palms to everyone you see, but you can still look them in the eye. As you smile, or say hello, or shake hands, in your mind you can still be offering them a lotus flower, a reminder of the Buddha nature in both of you.

The Two Keys to Compassionate Communication

We communicate to be understood and to understand others. If we're talking and no one is listening (maybe not even our own selves), we're not communicating effectively. There are two keys to effective and true communication. The first is deep listening. The second is loving speech. Deep listening and loving speech are the best instruments I know for establishing and restoring communication with others and relieving suffering.

We all want to be understood. When we interact with another person, particularly if we haven't practiced mindfulness of our own suffering and listened well to our own selves, we're anxious for others to understand us right away. We want to begin by expressing ourselves. But talking first like that doesn't usually work. Deep listening needs to come first. Practicing mindfulness of suffering—recognizing and embracing the suffering in oneself and in the other person—will give rise to the understanding necessary for good communication.

When we listen to someone with the intention of helping that person suffer less, this is deep listening. When we listen with compassion, we don't get caught in judgment. A judgment may form, but we don't hold on to it. Deep listening has the power to help us create a moment of joy, a moment of happiness, and to help us handle a painful emotion.

Now Is the Time to Listen Only

Deep listening is a wonderful practice. If you can listen for thirty minutes with compassion, you can help the other person suffer much less. If you don't practice mindfulness of compassion, you can't listen long. Mindfulness of compassion means you listen with only one intention—to help the other person suffer less. Your intention may be sincere, but if you haven't first practiced listening to yourself, and you don't practice mindfulness of compassion, you may rather quickly lose your ability to listen.

The other person may say things that are full of wrong perceptions, bitterness, accusation, and blaming. If we don't practice mindfulness, their words will set off irritation, judgment, and anger in us, and we will lose our capacity to listen compassionately. When irritation or anger arises, we lose our capacity to listen. That's why we have to practice, so that during the whole time of listening, compassion can remain in our hearts. If we can keep our compassion alive, the seeds of anger and judgment in our hearts will not be watered and spring up. We have to train ourselves first so we're able to listen to the other person.

It is okay if you're not ready to listen at a certain moment. If the quality of your listening is not good enough, it's better to pause and continue another day;

don't push yourself too hard. Practice mindful breathing and mindful walking until you're ready to really listen to the other person. You can say, "I want to listen to you when I'm at my best. Would it be all right if we continued tomorrow?"

Then, when we are ready to listen deeply, we can listen without interrupting. If we try to interrupt or correct the other person, we will transform the session into a debate and it will ruin everything. After we have deeply listened and allowed the other person to express everything in his heart, we'll have a chance later on to give him a little of the information he needs to correct his perception—but not now. Now we just listen, even if the person says things that are wrong. It's the practice of mindfulness of compassion that keeps us listening deeply.

You have to take the time to look and see the suffering in the other person. You must be prepared. Deep listening has only one purpose: to help others suffer less. Even if the person says wrong things, expresses bitterness, or blames, continue to listen compassionately for as long as you can. You may want to say this to yourself as a reminder:

I am listening to this person with only one purpose:
to give this person a chance to suffer less.

Keep the one purpose of deep listening alive in your heart and in your mind. As long as you are inhabited by the energy of compassion, you are safe. Even if what the other person says contains a lot of wrong perceptions, bitterness, anger, blame, and accusation, you are really safe.

Remember that the other person's speech may be based on prejudices and misunderstandings. You will have a chance later to offer some information so that he or she can correct his or her perception, but not now. Now is the time only to listen. If you can keep your mindfulness of compassion alive for even thirty minutes, you are inhabited by the energy of compassion and you are safe. As long as compassion is present, you can listen with equanimity.

You know that the other person is suffering. When we don't know how to handle the suffering inside us, we continue to suffer, and we make people around us suffer. When other people don't know how to handle their suffering, they become its victim. If you imbibe their judgment, fear, and anger, you become its second victim. But if you can listen deeply, understanding that what they are saying is coming from suffering, then you are protected by your compassion.

You only want to help them suffer less. You don't blame or judge them anymore.

Love Is Born from Understanding

Listening deeply and compassionately, you begin to understand the other person more fully, and love is nourished. The foundation of love is understanding, and that means first of all understanding suffering. Each of us is hungry for understanding. If you really want to love someone and make him or her happy, you have to understand that person's suffering. With understanding, your love will deepen and become true love. Listening to suffering is an essential ingredient for generating understanding and love.

I define happiness as the capacity to understand and to love, because without understanding and love no happiness could be possible. We don't have enough understanding and love, which is why we suffer so much. That is what we are thirsting for.

Compassion and love are born from understanding. How can you love unless you understand? How can the father love his son if he doesn't understand the suffering and difficulties of his son? How can someone make his beloved happy without knowing anything about that person's suffering and difficulties?

Do I Understand You Enough?

If you want to make someone happy, you should ask yourself the question "Do I understand him enough?" "Do I understand her enough?" Many people are reluctant to talk because they fear that what they say will be misunderstood. There are people who suffer so much; they're not capable of telling us about the suffering inside. And we have the impression that nothing is wrong—until it's too late.

Waiting has serious consequences. People may isolate themselves, they may suddenly end a friendship or relationship, and they may even commit suicide. Something had been bothering that person for a long time, but he or she pretended that everything was okay. Maybe fear or pride gets in the way. Listening and looking with mindfulness and concentration, we may discover that there's a block of suffering in that person. We see that she has suffered so much and doesn't know how to handle the suffering inside. So she continues to suffer and make other people suffer, too. Once you have seen that, suddenly your anger is no longer there. Compassion arises. You have the insight that she is suffering and needs help, not punishment.

If you need to, you can ask for help. You can say, "Dear One, I want to understand you more. I want to understand your difficulties and your suffering. I want to listen to you because I want to love you." When we take the time to look more deeply, we may see for the first time the big block of suffering in that person. Someone might pretend not to suffer, but that's not true. When you're able to listen compassionately, other people have a chance to tell you about their difficulties.

In any relationship, you may want to check whether you have understood the other person. If it is a relationship that is harmonious, in which communication is good, then happiness is there. If communication and harmony exist, it means mutual understanding is there. Don't wait until the other person has left or is full of anger to ask the important question "Do you think I understand you enough?" The other person will tell you if you haven't understood enough. He will know if you're able to listen with compassion. You may say, "Please tell me, please help me. Because I know very well that if I don't understand you, I will make a lot of mistakes." That is the language of love.

The question "Do you think I understand you enough?" is not just for romantic relationships, but for friends, family members, and anyone you care about. It can even help in a work setting. If you live with a family member, a romantic partner, or a friend, you may think that because you see this person every day you know a lot about him or her. But that's not correct. You know only a little about that person. You may have lived with someone for five, ten, or twenty years. But you may not have looked deeply into that person to understand him or her. You may have done the same with yourself. You have lived with yourself your whole life. We think that we already understand who we are. But unless we have listened deeply to ourselves, with compassion and curiosity and without judgment, we may not know ourselves very well at all.

If you wait until family members pass away, it will be too late to ask them to share more about themselves. It's nice when a child of any age sits with a parent and asks about their experiences, sufferings, and sources of happiness. Just sit and listen. With mindful breathing and listening to ourselves, our capacity for listening and looking expands deeply, and we may find the opportunity for much greater communication and connection with our parents and our loved ones.

When you see that the other person has suffering inside, compassion is born in your heart. You may want to do something to help that person suffer less. Your compassionate listening and loving speech will already do a lot to change the situation. Then you can sit with the person and together get insight into what other concrete actions, if any, are necessary to help the situation. Compassionate listening isn't the only thing we can do when someone is suffering, but it's almost always the first step.

Loving Speech

When you have to tell people bad news, telling the truth can be difficult. If you don't speak mindfully, the other person can get very angry or anxious after hearing your "truth." We can train ourselves to speak the truth in such a way that, in the end, the other person can accept it.

When you speak, you try to tell others the truth about your suffering and their suffering, this is loving speech. You speak in a way that helps others recognize the suffering inside themselves and in you. We have to be skillful. The one who speaks has to be very mindful, using words in a way that can help the listener not be caught in wrong perceptions. And the listener has to be careful not to be caught in the words being said or the ideas being offered. There needs to be mindfulness and skillfulness on the part of both the speaker and the listener.

Because you have first practiced compassionate listening, you know that what you say can carry with it insight and understanding. With more understanding, you can really help the other person suffer less, and your communication is more effective. You speak gently because you are willing to help. The way we communicate already makes the other person feel much better.

The words we say are nourishment. We can use words that will nourish ourselves and nourish another person. What you say, what you write, should convey only compassion and understanding. Your words can inspire confidence and openness in another person. Generosity can be practiced wonderfully with loving speech. You don't have to spend any money to practice generosity. In Buddhism another way of saying loving speech is Right Speech. In our daily life, Right Speech is what nourishes us and nourishes those around us.

Wrong Speech

We call loving speech "Right Speech" because we know that suffering is brought about by wrong speech. Our speech can cause a lot of suffering with unkind, untruthful, or violent words. Wrong speech is the kind of speech that lacks openness and does not have understanding, compassion, and reconciliation at its base.

When we write a note or a letter, when we speak on

the telephone, what we write or say should be Right Speech that conveys our insight, our understanding, and our compassion. When we practice Right Speech, we feel wonderful in our bodies and our minds. And the one who listens to us also feels wonderful. It's possible for us to use Right Speech, the speech of compassion, tolerance, and forgiveness, several times a day. It doesn't cost anything and it's very healing.

The Four Elements of Right Speech

Loving, truthful speech can bring a lot of joy and peace to people. But producing loving speech takes practice because we aren't used to it. When we hear so much speech that causes craving, insecurity, and anger, we get accustomed to speaking that way. Truthful, loving speech is something we need to train ourselves in.

In Buddhism there's a practice called the Ten Bodhisattva Trainings. Four of these ten relate to Right Speech. A bodhisattva is an enlightened being who has dedicated his or her life to alleviating the suffering of all living beings.

Enlightenment is always enlightenment about something. If you begin to understand the nature and the root of your suffering, that is a kind of enlightenment, and it helps you suffer less right away. There are those of us who are very critical of ourselves. That's because we haven't understood our own suffering. When we become a bodhisattva for ourselves, we don't blame ourselves or others anymore.

A bodhisattva is someone who can speak with gentle, loving speech and who can listen with compassion. Anyone can become a bodhisattva by training diligently. You don't have to practice for ten years to become a bodhisattva. Spend at least some time each day, even if it's only five or ten minutes, sitting, practicing mindful breathing, and listening to yourself.

Here are the four bodhisattva guidelines of the Ten Bodhisattva Trainings for Right Speech:

1. Tell the truth. Don't lie or turn the truth upside down.
2. Don't exaggerate.
3. Be consistent. This means no double-talk: speaking about something in one way to one person and in an opposite way to another for selfish or manipulative reasons.
4. Use peaceful language. Don't use insulting or violent words, cruel speech, verbal abuse, or condemnation.

Tell the Truth

The first element of Right Speech is to tell the truth. We don't lie. We try not to say untruthful things. If we think the truth is too shocking, we find a skillful and loving way to tell the truth. But we have to respect the truth. There are those who verbally abuse people and make them suffer, and then say, "I'm only telling the truth." But they tell the "truth" in a violent and attacking way. Sometimes it can even cause the other person to feel great suffering.

When you tell the truth, sometimes the result isn't what you wanted. You need to look deep into the mind of the other person to see how you can tell the truth in such a way that others don't feel threatened, so they can listen. You try to tell the truth in a loving and protective way. It's important to remember that what you think is the truth could be your own incomplete or erroneous perception. You think it's the truth, but your perception may be partial; it may be blocked by something.

Lying is dangerous, because one day the other person may find out the truth. That could be a catastrophe. So if we don't want to lie, and we don't want to trigger a hurt, we have to be mindful of our words and find a skillful means to tell the truth. There are many ways to tell the truth. It's an art.

The truth is a solid base for a long-lasting relationship. If you don't build your relationship on the truth, sooner or later it will crumble. We have to find the best way to tell the truth so that the other person can receive it easily. Sometimes even the most skillful words can cause pain. That is okay. Pain can heal. If your words are spoken with compassion and understanding, the pain will heal more quickly.

Suffering can be beneficial. There can be goodness in suffering, but we don't want to make the other person suffer needlessly. We can minimize the shock and the pain. We try to convey the truth in such a way that other people can hear us without suffering too much. The important thing is that they feel safe. They may not "get it," or it may take time for them to "get it." They may continue to have a different perception than ours.

Sometimes you can begin by telling another story, the story of someone else whose situation is similar to the person you are speaking to, so that he or she can get accustomed to the idea. It's easier to listen to the story of another person. You can say, "What do you think? Would it be good for the other person to hear the truth or not?" Usually people say, "Yes, it's good to hear the truth." Sometimes the person you are speaking to will come to the conclusion independently and learn from the case of the other person. It takes a lot of practice to tell the truth in a way that the other person can hear.

Don't Exaggerate

The second part of Right Speech is to refrain from inventing and exaggerating. You want to speak about some little thing, but you exaggerate and make it very big. For example, someone has made a mistake, but you exaggerate as though it's something many times worse. Sometimes when we're speaking to ourselves, we make something seem very tragic to justify and even feed anger. There may be some truth in what you want to say, but you exaggerate what the other person has done, so you paint a wrong image of the other. This may seem harmless, but it takes you away from the truth and takes away the trust in a relationship.

Be Consistent

The third kind of incorrect speech is what we call in Vietnamese "forked tongue" or "double tongue." It means you say something to one person, but when speaking about the same matter to another person you say something different as a way of gaining some advantage. You speak about the same situation but in conflicting ways. This causes division and can make a person or group think badly about the other person or group when there's no basis for it. This can cause a lot of suffering on both sides and might even cause them to become enemies. Right Speech requires being true to your word and not changing the content for your own advantage or to portray yourself in a better light.

Use Peaceful Language

The fourth aspect of Right Speech is to refrain from speech that's violent, condemning, abusive, humiliating, accusing, or judgmental.

The Four Criteria

In the time of the Buddha, people were caught by mental constructions and interpreted the teachings in ways that were not intended by the teacher. The Buddha and his students came up with four criteria that should be contained in any teaching. These four criteria are helpful today in evaluating whether we and others are using Right Speech and speaking the truth effectively. The four criteria are:

1. We have to speak the language of the world.
2. We may speak differently to different people, in a way that reflects how they think and their ability to receive the teaching.
3. We give the right teaching according to person, time, and place, just as a doctor prescribes the right medicine.
4. We teach in a way that reflects the absolute truth.

The First Criterion: Speak the Language of the World

The first criterion is to understand the worldly way of seeing things, the worldly view. Sometimes we have to use the kind of language that people speak and the way they view things. If you don't use the language of the world, most people won't understand what you mean, and you can communicate only with people who already think like you. This doesn't mean you have to learn Vietnamese and Arabic, but rather that you have to speak in terms that people can understand, based on their daily experience of life.

For example, we are used to saying that the sky is "above" and the earth is "below." When we sit here, we say that what's above us is "up" and what's below us is "down." But for those who are sitting on the other side of the planet, our down is their up, and our up is their down. What is up and down for this corner of the planet is not up and down for another part of the planet. So "up and down" is a truth, but it's a relative truth. We can use it as part of our common language, to communicate with each other, without needing to have an extended discussion of "up" and "down" each time we talk.

The Second Criterion: Speak According to the Understanding of the Person Listening

The second criterion says that we may have to speak to each person differently. This doesn't contradict the element of Right Speech that says not to speak with a forked tongue (doublespeak). We need to keep the truthful content the same while being aware of the perspective and understanding of the person we're speaking to, so others have an opportunity to really hear what's being said. With one person you speak one way; with another person you have to speak a different way. You have to look deeply at the person to see how he or she perceives, and speak in a way that takes that into account, so others can understand what you say. If someone's understanding is profound, you speak in a way that takes that into consideration.

One day someone asked the Buddha, "When that person passes away, which heaven do you think he will go to?" The Buddha answered that he might be born into this or that heavenly realm. Later another person asked the Buddha, "When that person dies, where will he go?" The Buddha answered, "He will not go any-where." Someone standing nearby asked the Buddha why he had given the two people two different answers. The Buddha replied that it depends on the person who asks. He said, "I have to speak according to the mind of the person who listens and the ability of that person to receive what I share."

There's a story of someone who gave a woman a pot of milk in the morning. At the end of the day, he came to get it back. During the day the milk had turned into butter and cheese. The man said, "But I gave you milk, and you gave me back butter and cheese." So is milk the same as or different from the butter? It's not the same, but it's not different either.

To those with more profound understanding, you have to give a deeper answer, reflecting that nothing is permanent and everything is constantly changing. So the teaching you give and the way you speak depends on the degree of wisdom of the receiver and that person's ability to understand what you say. You speak according to the background and the abilities of the person you're speaking to.

The Third Criterion: Prescribe the Right Medicine for the Disease

The third criterion is to prescribe the right medicine for the disease. If you give someone the wrong medicine, that person could die. So to each you give a particular medicine. When you have attachment, craving, or despair, remember that you are your own teacher. You can listen to these strong emotions and communicate back the healing you need.

Don't think that if you hear or read something that inspires you, you should then repeat it word for word. Think of how to make these truths you heard resonate with your own. Similarly, you also have to know the mind and the background of the person you're speaking to. If you were to give another person exactly the teaching you heard, it might not be the appropriate teaching for that person. You have to adapt what you say to the other's background. But what you say must also reflect the true teaching. So you use worldly language, but not just any worldly language. Your language has to be appropriate to the situation, while not straying from the truth.

Think about how we talk to children about death or violence in the world. Do we tell them the truth in a different way than we would an adult? One time when I was visiting a museum, I entered a room containing a mummified human body. A little girl was there looking at the dead person. After we both had stood there looking together for a while, with fear in her eyes she asked me something like, "Am I going to be lying dead on a table one day?" I breathed in and out and gave her the only answer that was appropriate for that situation: "No." I hope that someday a wise parent or friend will be able to talk with her about the impermanence of all things, including our bodies *and* the deep teaching of the Buddha that nothing ever ceases to exist altogether, nothing goes from being existent to being nonexistent. But this was not the time or place for her to be told all that, so I gave her the best answer available under the circumstances, which was "no."

Even with adults, we can vary what we say depending on how fragile we think they might be about a certain subject. We want to share information in a way that people can integrate and use later, even if not right away. This isn't lying; it's telling the truth in a skillful way. There was a man belonging to the Jain tradition who asked the Buddha whether human beings have a self. The Buddha could have answered that there is no self, but he kept silent. Then the Jain man asked, "Then do we have *no* self?" The Buddha still kept silent. Later Ananda asked the Buddha, "Why didn't you say there is no self?" The Buddha said, "I know that he is caught in his view. If I were to say that there is no self, he would be lost and he would suffer a lot. So although 'no self' is correct according to our teaching, it was better to keep silent."

The Fourth Criterion: Reflect the Absolute Truth

The fourth criterion is the absolute truth, the most profound view of things, and it may be found in sentences such as "There is no separate self" or "There is no such thing as birth and death." The absolute truth is correct; it is the closest thing to a description of the ultimate reality, but it can make people feel lost if they haven't had a spiritual teacher who could skillfully convey its depths to them, in a way they could take in. So whenever we need to say something we know will be difficult for others to hear, we have to be humble and try to look more and more deeply to discover in what way we can talk about these things.

There are some absolute truths, such as that of no-birth and no-death, that are very difficult to grasp in our everyday way of thinking and everyday lives. But then if we are shown something simple, such as a cloud, we can grasp very easily that the cloud isn't "born" and it doesn't "die"; it simply changes form. We may think of these absolute truths as abstract, but they are visible all around us in the natural world if we look deeply or have a teacher or companion with whom we can talk about what we see.

If you use these four criteria, you will not be confused when you are reading or listening to something. They can also help you listen well to others and express yourself effectively in everyday life, whether in friendly conversation, when speaking to or listening in a group, or when reading a text, whether secular or religious. You will have a deep understanding of what is the truth in any given situation and how best to respond.

This training isn't just about how we speak but also goes along with how we listen. So the focus is what happens not only with the mind and tongue, but also with the ear. When we listen more deeply and see more clearly, compassion arises, and we use mindful speech that reflects our sincere and caring intentions. Instead of speaking cruelly, we begin to listen with compassion.

When we have the ability to listen with compassion to the suffering of the other person, we will benefit as well.

Our compassion makes us happy and peaceful. When we listen with compassion, we can understand things that we wouldn't be able to understand if we were full of anger.

Listening deeply is a kind of looking deeply. You look not with your eyes but with your ears. When you look with your eyes, you can see the suffering. When you look with your ears, you can hear the vibration of that person's words. In Vietnamese, the bodhisattva Avalok-iteshvara is called Quan The Am (in Chinese, Kwan Yin). *Quan* means to contemplate deeply; *the* means world; and *am* means sound. Quan The Am listens to all the sounds, all the suffering of the world. When you listen like that, compassion is born in you, and you can have peace. Please listen with great compassion. Even when you're sad because of bad news, your compassion will soothe your agitation and make you more peaceful.

Help People Understand

On my last trip to India, I was invited to be the guest editor for one day at the *Times of India*, the largest daily paper in India. It was during the Gandhi commemoration days in October 2008. One day I was sitting with the regular editors in a meeting when news came in of a terrorist attack in Mumbai, near the Pakistan border, in which a lot of people had been killed.

The editors asked me, "If you were a journalist in our time, how would you report when there is so much bad news and so little good news. How should we be as journalists?" It's a difficult question. Reporters have to report the news. But if journalists are writing only from the place of shock, fear, or outrage, they will report in a way that waters the fear and anger of the reader, possibly creating more violence. So what can we do when we receive such news?

I didn't answer right away. I went back to my in-breath and out-breath, and I kept silent for a time, and they kept silent too. Then I said, "You have to tell the truth. But you have to report in such a way that we don't water the seeds of fear, anger, and vengeance in people. So you have to sit as a practitioner and look deeply, and ask, 'Why would someone do violence to innocent people?'" When you've looked deeply, you will see that those who do violence have a wrong perception of the situation. They're so sure their perception is the truth. And they may think that if they also die in the explosion, they will go directly to heaven to join God.

Everybody wants to live; nobody wants to die. But they may think that by killing others and dying themselves they are doing the work of God. They think that those on the other side are the enemies of God. You can see that is wrong thinking, and so you have great compassion for them. For whoever has such a view, life is very dark and he suffers a lot. There are many wrong perceptions everywhere. So long as those wrong perceptions persist, the number of terrorists will only increase. It will be very difficult to find and control them all.

If one terrorist group is violently destroyed, another will emerge; it's endless. So I told the editors, "When you report on terrorist acts, use your compassion and deep understanding. Explain the story in such a way that the reader doesn't become enraged and perhaps become another terrorist."

We can tell the truth, but we must help people understand. When people understand, their anger will lessen. They don't lose hope, they know what to do and what not to do, what to consume and what not to consume in order not to continue this kind of suffering. So my message that morning was that we should reflect and discuss events in a way that will not increase the despair and the anger in people. Instead, we can help them to understand why things happen, so their insight and compassion increase. We can make a big difference with the practice of looking deeply. The solution isn't to hide the truth.

Using Right Speech in Daily Life

The four trainings in Right Speech remind us every day to use words that express nondiscrimination, forgiveness, understanding, support, and love. It's very liberating to be able to say or write something using compassionate speech. Speaking in this way is as healing for the speaker as it is for the person being spoken to. These four trainings also remind us that anything we say which contains poisons, discrimination, and hate will make us suffer and make others suffer. It's a simple equation: wrong speech causes ill-being. Right Speech brings about well-being and healing. Every day we can say something that has the capacity to heal and help people. A grown-up can do this. A child can do this. A businessperson, a politician, or a teacher can do this. We don't need to wait for a special moment. We can stop what we are doing right now and send an e-mail that contains Right Speech, and we can relieve the suffering inside us and the suffering in others right away.

4

The Six Mantras of Loving Speech

When we have the impression that we're all alone and nobody supports us, we can remember that it's only a perception. It's not accurate. Think of a tree standing outside right now. The tree is supporting us with beauty, freshness, and oxygen for us to breathe. That kind of support is also a kind of love. The fresh air outside, the plants that feed us, and the water that flows over our hands from the tap all support us.

There are many ways that people can support us and love us without actually saying, "I love you." You may know people who have never said, "I love you," but you know they love you. When I was ordained as a novice monk, I had a teacher who I knew loved me deeply, but he never said, "I love you." That is the traditional way. If one pronounced the words "I love you," it seemed that some of the sacredness was lost. Sometimes we feel very grateful, but we want to express our gratefulness in ways other than simply saying, "thank you." Look for the many ways people communicate their love without saying it. Maybe, like the tree, they are supporting you in other ways.

It's also true that the people you love may not know you love them. Sometimes we want to tell someone how much we care, but we don't know the words to say it so that person will understand how we feel.

The Six Mantras are six sentences that embody loving speech and let people know that you see them, you understand them, and you care for them. In Buddhism we call these sentences "mantras." They're a kind of magic formula. When you pronounce them, you can bring about a miracle, because happiness becomes available right away.

As with each practice, you begin with mindful breathing to bring about your true presence. Then you come to the other person in mindfulness, committed to the practice of compassionate communication. You may want to breathe in and out three times before you say the mantra. We need those three breaths in and out. This will make you calm, and your calm will be communicated to the other person. Then, when you go to another person, you know you will be fresh, you will have peace, and you can offer those things to the other person.

If you want the mantra to work, you have to breathe in

mindfully first and become fresh before you pronounce it. You look into the other person's eyes, and you say these short sentences. A mantra may contain as few as four words, but in these words you are able to be fully there for the person you love.

The First Mantra

The first mantra is: "I am here for you." This is the best gift you can give a loved one. Nothing is more precious than your presence. No matter how expensive the things you buy for someone else, they're not as precious as your true presence. That wonderful presence is fresh, solid, free, and calm, and you offer it to your loved ones to increase their happiness and your own happiness. "I am here for you."

To love someone means to be there for him or for her. To be there is an art and a practice. Are you truly there for the person you love, one hundred percent? Using the skills of mindful breathing and mindful walking, you can bring together your body and mind to restore yourself and produce your true presence in the here and the now. To be there like that, for yourself and for the other person, is an act of love.

We can also use this mantra with ourselves. When I

73

say to myself, "I am here for you," it also means that I am there for myself. My mind goes home to my body, and I become aware that I have a body. That is a practice of love, directed to yourself. If you are capable of being with yourself, you are capable of being with the person you love.

The practice can be very pleasant. Breathing in and bringing your mind home to your body can be a very pleasant thing to do. You enjoy your in-breath, you enjoy your body, and you enjoy your mind. Then the mantra will have an effect on those around you too.

You don't need to wait for the practice to be reciprocated. The other person doesn't need to say anything in return. When you produce the mantra, both of you benefit. The mantra helps you and the other person come home to yourselves and to the moment you are sharing. So the effect is double.

We say that love is based on understanding. But how can you understand someone if you aren't present? Your mind has to be in the here and the now before you can love. So the first definition of love is to be there. How can you love if you are not there? To love you have to be there. The tree outside your window is there, supporting you. You can be there for yourself and for your loved ones, just like the tree. Mindfulness practice is the foundation of your love. You cannot love properly and deeply without mindfulness.

Although you're saying, "I am here for you," the other person doesn't have to be there for you to practice the first mantra. If the other person is at home or at work, you can use the phone. As you hold the phone in your hand, breathe in and out a few times to make yourself present and calm. When you hear the phone ringing, you can continue your mindful breathing. When the other person picks up the phone, you can ask if he or she has a moment. If so, you can just say: "I am here for you." If you have practiced mindful breathing, the way you say the mantra will convey your calm and your presence.

The Second Mantra

Don't use the second mantra until you have practiced the first and produced your presence. Then, when you are truly there in the here and the now, you are in a position to recognize the presence of the other person. The second mantra is: "I know you are there, and I am very happy." You are letting your loved one know that his or her presence is important to your happiness.

The second mantra acknowledges that you really see the other person. This is crucial, because when a person ignores you, you don't feel that you are loved. You may feel that the people you love are too busy to see you. Your loved one may be driving the car and thinking of everything except you who are sitting in the next seat. You don't have that person's attention. To love means to be aware of the presence of your beloved one and to recognize that presence as something very precious to you. You use the energy of mindfulness to recognize and embrace the presence of your beloved one. Embraced by your mindfulness, the other person will bloom like a flower.

"I know you are there, and I am very happy." The second mantra is to reaffirm the presence of the other person as someone very important to you. The second mantra, like the first, only works if you breathe in and out before saying it. Imagine the other person is not there; he or she has moved away or passed on. You might feel a big hole. Right now that person is alive and near you, so you're very lucky. That's why you have to practice the second mantra to remind yourself of the gift of that person's presence.

When someone says he loves you but he ignores your presence and doesn't pay attention to your being there, you don't have the feeling that you are loved. So when you love someone you have to recognize his or her presence as something precious to you. The second mantra can be practiced every day, several times a day. "I know you are there, and it makes me very happy."

This mantra, like the first, can be shared anytime—before work, at the dinner table, or over the phone or by e-mail if you want to share it with someone you don't get a chance to see. These mantras feel a bit awkward at first, while you're getting used to them, but once you see the results, they will get easier. You can make yourself and the other person happy right away. It's quicker than instant coffee! But remember one thing: a mantra can be practiced successfully only if you know how to make yourself present and say it in mindfulness.

The Third Mantra

While the first two mantras can be said several times a day, no matter what the situation, the third mantra is used when you notice that the other person is suffering. The third mantra can help the other person suffer less right away. The third mantra is: "I know you suffer, and that is why I am here for you."

Thanks to your mindfulness, you know that something is not going well with your friend or loved one. When your loved one is suffering, your impulse may be to want to do something to fix it, but you don't need to do much.

You just need to be there for him or her. That is true love. True love is made of mindfulness.

Because of your mindfulness, you know when something is not going well with a loved one. When you notice that, you want to do something to help him or her suffer less. You don't have to do anything other than to be there. When you say the mantra, right away your loved one will suffer less.

When you suffer and your loved ones ignore your suffering, you suffer much more. But if the other person is aware of your suffering and offers his presence to you during those difficult moments, you suffer less right away. It doesn't take much time to bring relief. So please use this mantra in your relationship to help the other person suffer less.

The Fourth Mantra

The fourth mantra is a little more difficult, especially for those of us with a lot of pride. You use the fourth mantra when you suffer and you believe that the other person has caused your suffering. This happens from time to time. If it was someone you didn't care as much about who had said or done that to you, you would have suffered less. But when someone you love says something that feels critical or dismissive, you suffer deeply. If we suffer, and we don't look deeply into our suffering and find compassion for ourselves and the other person, we may want to punish the person who hurt us because he or she has dared to make us suffer. When we suffer, we think it's the other person's fault for not appreciating us enough or loving us enough. Many of us have a natural tendency to want to punish the other person. One way we think of punishing the other person is to show that we can survive without him or her.

Many of us have made this mistake. I myself have also made that mistake. But we learn. We want to show the other person that without him or her we can survive very well. This is an indirect way of saying, "I don't need you." But that's not true. In fact when we suffer, we need others.

When we suffer, we should tell others that we suffer and that we need their help. We usually do the opposite. We don't want to go and ask for help. That's why we need the fourth mantra: "I suffer, please help."

It's so simple, and it's also a little bit difficult. But if you can bring yourself to pronounce the mantra, right away you suffer less. I guarantee it. So please write that sentence down on a piece of paper the size of a credit card and put it in your wallet. It's a magic formula: "I suffer. Please help."

If you don't practice this mantra, you may be sulking; if others notice that something is wrong, that maybe you suffer, they might try to comfort you and say, "Are you suffering?" When someone asks you this, you might have the tendency to respond, "Suffer? Why should I be suffering?" You know that's not the truth. You suffer deeply, yet you pretend you don't suffer. You're being untruthful as a way of punishing the other person. If he or she tries to come close and put a hand on your shoulder, you may want to snap, "Leave me alone. I can survive very well without you." Many of us commit that kind of mistake. But we can learn.

Practicing the mantra, you do the opposite. You have to recognize that you suffer. The mantra can also be a little longer, if that feels more appropriate to the situation: "I suffer. I want you to know it. I don't understand why you did or said what you did. So please explain. I need your help." That is true love. To say, "I don't suffer; I don't need your help" is not the language of true love.

The next time you suffer, and you believe it's the other person's fault and that she is the cause of your suffering, remember to take out the paper and read it, and you will know exactly what to do—practice the fourth mantra.

According to our practice in Plum Village, you have the right to suffer twenty-four hours but not more. There's a deadline. The deadline is twenty-four hours, and you have to practice the fourth mantra before the deadline. You have your phone. You have your computer. I'm sure that when you are able to bring yourself to write it down, you will suffer less right away. If you aren't calm enough within twenty-four hours to practice the fourth mantra, you can write it down on a piece of paper and leave it on the other person's desk or somewhere it is sure to be seen.

The mantra can be further broken down into three sentences. The first is: "I suffer and I want you to know." That's sharing yourself with the person you care about. You share your happiness with each other; you also need to share your suffering.

The second sentence is: "I am doing my best." It means, "I am practicing mindfulness, and when I get angry I won't say anything that can cause damage to myself or to you. I am practicing mindful breathing, mindful walking, and looking deeply into my suffering to find the roots of my suffering. I believe that you have caused my suffering, but I know I shouldn't be too sure about that. I'm looking to see whether my suffering has come from a wrong perception on my part. Maybe you didn't mean to say it. Maybe you didn't want to do it. I'm now doing my best to practice looking deeply, to recognize my anger and embrace it tenderly."

The second sentence is an invitation for the other person to do the same, to practice like you are. When the other person gets the message, he might say to himself, "Oh, I didn't know that she was suffering. What have I done or said to make her suffer like that?" It is an invitation for the other person to also practice looking deeply. If one of you finds out the cause, that person should communicate right away and apologize for being unskillful so that the other person doesn't continue to suffer.

So the second sentence is an invitation for both sides to look deeply, to be aware of what is going on and investigate the real cause of the suffering. It's a recognition that the other person is human and is doing his or her best at the time, and that we are doing our best as well.

The third sentence is: "Please help." This sentence acknowledges that we can't figure it all out on our own. We need each other. This is perhaps the hardest part. The three sentences together are: "I suffer, and I want you to know it. I am doing my best. Please help."

The Fifth Mantra

The fifth mantra is: "This is a happy moment." When you are with someone you care about, you can use this mantra. This is not autosuggestion or wishful thinking, because there are conditions of happiness that are there. If we're not mindful, we won't recognize them. This mantra is to remind ourselves and the other person that we are very lucky, that there are so many conditions of happiness that are available in the here and the now. We can breathe easily. We have each other. We have the blue sky and the solidity of the whole earth supporting us. Sitting with the other person, walking together, you may want to pronounce the fifth mantra and realize how lucky you are.

Being able to recognize that this moment is a happy moment depends on your mindfulness. These conditions of happiness are more than enough for both of you to be happy in the here and the now. It is mindfulness that makes the present moment into a wonderful moment. We can each learn how to bring happiness into the here and the now with our practice. What are we waiting for to be happy? Why do we have to wait? With mindfulness you can recognize that it *is* possible to be happy right here and right now.

The Sixth Mantra

You use the sixth mantra when someone praises or criticizes you. You can use it equally well in both cases. The sixth mantra is: "You are partly right."

I have weaknesses in me, and I have strengths in me. If you praise me, I shouldn't get too puffed up and ignore the fact that in me there are also challenges. When you criticize me, I shouldn't get lost in that and ignore the positive things.

When you see beautiful things in someone, you tend to overlook the things that are not so beautiful. But as human beings, we all have both positive and negative aspects. So when your loved one rhapsodizes about you, telling you that you are the very image of perfection, you can say, "You are partly right. You know that I have other things in me too." In this way you retain your humility. You don't become the victim of a prideful illusion, because you know that you're not perfect. This is very important. When you pronounce the sixth mantra, you preserve your humility.

If the other person criticizes you, you can reply, "Darling, you are only partly right, because I also have good things in me." Without judgment, you investigate so you can improve. If somebody misjudges you, you reply, "You have said something that is partly correct. But in me there are also positive things." Likewise, when someone admires you, you can thank them for appreciating you but also point out that they are seeing one part of you and that you have many challenges too. "You have said something that's only partly correct, because I have many weaknesses that you perhaps haven't seen yet." If someone says, "You have many weaknesses," you can say, "You are partly correct. I have strengths too." You may answer them that way in silence or say it nicely. "You are only seeing part of me, not the totality. I have other things in me that are much better."

The sixth mantra is the truth. You don't lie, and you don't fall into false humility. You just say it, either aloud or silently to yourself. Inside you there are many wonderful qualities and many weaknesses; you accept both. But that acceptance doesn't prevent you from developing your positive qualities and addressing your weaknesses.

We can use the same method when we look at other people. We can accept others like we accept ourselves. We know that what they are expressing is only part of them. Before judging and shouting at somebody, instead of telling someone he or she has no value, we have to look deeper. I know people who are very sensitive. Even a slight judgment makes them weep and become very unhappy. Perhaps you also know people like this. So we accept ourselves with all our weaknesses, and then we have peace. We don't judge ourselves; we accept. I have these qualities and these weaknesses, but I will try to improve slowly, at my speed. If you can look at yourself like that, you can look at others like that too, without judgment.

Even if that person has many weaknesses, he also has many talents, many positive things. No one is without positive qualities. So when others judge you wrongly, you have to say that they are partly right but they have not seen the other parts of you. The other person only sees part of you, not the totality, so you don't have to be unhappy at all.

We can use these six mantras to make a close relationship stronger. My friend Elizabeth recently shared several ways in which she has used the mantras. Her sister is one year older than she is. They were always together growing up, but over the years and especially as they grew into young adults, Elizabeth had gotten in the habit of lecturing her sister a little and telling her what to do. As you can imagine, sometimes her sister had strong reactions.

With the practice of mindfulness, Elizabeth said, she became more aware of what she was saying, and she realized the importance of changing that habit. When she visited her sister, she started practicing her version of the second mantra, saying: "I'm really happy that you're here." She got in touch with, and expressed, a heartfelt appreciation of her sister's presence in her life, and of the fact that her sister was doing the best she could.

Elizabeth also used the mantras in her marriage. In the beginning, whenever her husband said something that really hurt her, she immediately had the desire to punish. She tried instead slowly going to him and using her version of the fourth mantra, asking him, "You said this thing to me that I really don't understand. What was that about?" He would share, and most times, she discovered that his remark was nothing about her really. It was often something else entirely that was going on. The mantra "opened up a door" for her "to see what was happening in his world."

Sometimes, Elizabeth would say something to her husband, and he'd have a strong reaction, and she'd react to his reaction. Eventually she learned to instead practice the third mantra—"I know you suffer; that's why I'm here for you"—by asking him, "Was it something I said? I really want to understand what happened. I'm sorry. I don't mean to say or do things that are hurtful. If you let me know, I can understand how the things I say affect you."

She also told me about one particular time during her stay in Plum Village. She was in the courtyard garden, harvesting the petals of rose blossoms that were just beginning to droop, to use for tea. A gardener came along and scolded Elizabeth for taking away flowers that were grow-ing there for everyone to enjoy in the courtyard. Elizabeth said, "I'm not taking the fresh ones, only the fading ones." But the gardener was not appeased. Elizabeth went to ask the advice of one of our nuns who she knew could help her understand. The sister shared with her that lately some other people had been picking flowers from the garden for their own use, and the gardener had a sensitivity about that. "Elizabeth," the sister said, "you just bumped into his sensitivity." After she heard that, Elizabeth was able to go to the gardener and practice the third mantra. She said, "I understand the situation better now, and I won't touch the flowers in the courtyard if you prefer." The gardener was getting ready to go away on a trip to Germany, and Elizabeth also practiced the first mantra—"I'm here for you"—by telling him that during his absence, she would water the roses and trim the rosehips for him.

Another friend recently shared that he was suffering a lot during a retreat. He chose to practice the fourth mantra—"I suffer; please help"—by sharing with his roommates that he didn't need to talk about anything, just to be allowed space. This allowed his roommates to understand what was happening with him, not take it personally, and be more accepting when he wasn't able to be there for them as they would like. It was beneficial to see what he needed and for him to ask for that support.

The Six Mantras are something that everyone can practice at home. Children can do them too. So often children feel powerless in the family. But with mindfulness, concentration, and practice of the Six Mantras, they have a tool. By saying a mantra with love and full presence, a child can change the situation—even a tense one—right away. It also gives parents a chance to use the language of love instead of authority when communicating with their children. This keeps communication alive between parents and children. When there's no real communication in the family, both parents and children suffer. The practice of the Six Mantras is a way to use loving speech and deep listening to keep the door of communication open. With this kind of communication, we will understand each other better, and then our love will be true love because it will be based on understanding.

Bringing Compassionate Communication to Your Relationships

When you are able to use the Six Mantras with your loved ones, you will find that you are building a kind of home together. By listening compassionately to yourself, you have started to come home to yourself. With compassionate communication, you can help your loved ones come home to themselves. Your loved ones are also looking for home—for some warmth and a refuge. Once you have a home, you can help the other person. You are confident because you know how to connect with yourself and make a home for yourself. Your confidence can inspire others to do the same. They may find a home in you, and then lean on that to build a home in themselves.

You don't need an iPhone to do this. You need your eyes, to look at them with compassion. You need your ears and your mouth to listen with compassion and speak mindfully. When your loved one is able to go back to himself or herself, then your relationship becomes a real relationship, because both of you feel at home in yourselves. Don't be afraid to give your loved ones the space they need to listen to themselves. When you have enough space to listen to your own self, when you come together, you find a home in each other as well as in yourselves. There is a communal home for you to share. This becomes the base of all your relationships. If you want to help society, your community, your country, you have to have a home base. When you have a true home in yourself and in your home, you have happiness, safety, and fulfillment. Then you are in a position to go out and help create a more compassionate and loving community.

5

When Difficulties Arise

Many of us suffer because our communication with other people is difficult. At work, for example, we often feel we have tried everything and there is no way to reach our colleagues. This is often true in families as well. We feel our parents, our siblings, or our children are too stuck in their ways. We think no real communication is possible.

Yet there are many ways to reconcile and to create openings for more compassionate communication.

Communicating When You're Angry

One reason we have trouble communicating with others is that we often try to communicate when we are angry. We suffer, and we don't want to be alone with all that suffering. We believe that we are angry because of something others did, and we want them to know it. Anger has urgency to it. We want to let others know right away what the problem with them is.

But when we're angry, we aren't lucid. Acting while angry can lead to a lot of suffering and can escalate the situation. That doesn't mean we should suppress our anger. We shouldn't pretend that everything is fine when it isn't. It's possible to feel and engage with our anger in a healthy and compassionate manner. When anger is there, we should handle it with tenderness because our anger is us. We shouldn't do violence to our anger. Doing violence to our anger is doing violence to ourselves.

Mindful breathing helps us recognize our anger and treat it tenderly. Mindful energy embraces the energy of anger. Anger is a strong energy, and we may need to sit with it for a while. When you cook potatoes, you have to maintain the fire underneath for at least fifteen or twenty minutes. The same is true of the practice of mindfulness when it embraces anger. It will take a while, because the anger takes a while to cook.

After you have sat with mindful awareness and calmed your anger, you can look deeply into the anger to see its nature and where it has come from. What is the root of that anger? Anger may come from a wrong perception or a habitual way of responding to events that doesn't reflect our deepest values.

In popular psychotherapy, we're sometimes encouraged to express our anger physically to "get it out of our system." We're advised to allow our anger to manifest by shouting in a secluded place or hitting an inanimate substitute, such as a pillow.

I haven't found this practice to be useful in transforming the roots of anger. Think of a woodstove. If something goes wrong with it, you can open the windows so the smoke goes out. But if the stove still has that defect, the smoke will come again. You have to fix the woodstove. Yelling and punching your pillow can be just rehearsing and nourishing anger and making it stronger, not getting it out of your system.

You have to get genuinely in touch with your anger in order to heal. While you're hitting your pillow, you're not really getting in touch with your anger in a way that helps your understanding grow. You're not even getting in touch with the pillow, because if you were in touch with the pillow, you would know that it was only a pillow.

Suppressing anger can be dangerous. It will explode if it is ignored. Anger, like all strong emotions, wants to express itself. So how do we handle it? The best thing is to go home to ourselves and take care of our anger. We can remember the first mantra and be there for ourselves and take care of our anger. We return to ourselves and connect body and mind. Return to your practice of mindful breathing and mindful walking. To be present means to be mindful and then use that mindfulness to recognize, embrace, and look deeply at our strong emotions.

Usually when anger manifests, we want to confront the person we think is the source of our anger. We're more interested in setting that person straight than in taking care of the more urgent matter, which is our own anger. We are like the person whose house is on fire who goes chasing after the arsonist instead of going home to put out the fire. Meanwhile, the house continues to burn.

There are many things you can do to communicate that you are suffering over something that somebody has done. You can write a note or send an e-mail to the person. But first practice mindful breathing and take care of your anger. This is a perfect time to use the fourth mantra: "I suffer. Please help." You may phone the other person once you have calmed your anger, but only when you can calmly tell him or her that you suffer and you want help. You can let the other person know that you are doing your best to take care of your suffering. Encourage that person to do the same. Asking for help when we're angry is very difficult, but it allows others to see your suffering instead of just your anger. They will see that suffering causes the anger, and then communication and healing can begin.

Helping Each Other Suffer Less

When we have a rift or an estrangement from someone we care about, both people suffer. If we didn't care deeply about the other person, the rift would not be so painful. It's the people we care most about who trigger our greatest suffering. We may spend a long time living with the rift, until we start to think of it as irreparable.

But as long as it's there, we'll always be trying to avoid it, to cover it up, because we are afraid to be in touch with the suffering inside. We can pretend that it's not there, but it's really there, a big block inside.

The suffering in us demands to be understood. With our daily practice, we can generate enough mindfulness and be strong enough to come home to our suffering without fear. Mindfulness helps us recognize suffering inside. Mindfulness helps us embrace that suffering, which is the first step.

When someone has caused you a lot of pain, you may not even want to look at or be in the same room as that person, because you will suffer. With awareness, you can understand your own suffering and recognize the suffering in the other person. You may even understand that the reason that person suffers so much is because he or she doesn't know how to handle the suffering. His suffering spills out, and you are its victim. Maybe he doesn't want to make you suffer, but he doesn't know another way. He can't understand and transform his suffering, and so he makes the people around him suffer too, even when that's not his intention. Because he suffers, you suffer. He doesn't need punishment; he needs help.

You can help by acknowledging the suffering in him. If there is some difficulty in a relationship, we have to acknowledge the difficulty. It's tempting to say that everything is okay, because the difficulty can feel overwhelming. But without acknowledging the difficulty, we can't generate understanding and compassion, and we feel alienated. We can't help.

You have to use the tools of compassionate communication, the deep listening and loving speech you have practiced, to restore communication with the person with whom you are having difficulty. After a short period of mindful breathing, you can say something like this to the other person:

"I know you're not feeling too happy right now."

"In the past I didn't understand your feelings, so I reacted in a way that made you suffer more, and that also made me suffer more. I wasn't able to help you resolve the problem. I reacted angrily in a way that has made the situation worse."

"It's not my intention to make you suffer. It's because I didn't understand your suffering, and I didn't understand my suffering either."

"I understand my difficult feelings better now, and I also want to understand yours. Understanding your suffering, your difficulties, will help me behave in a way that can be more helpful."

"If you care for me, help me understand."

"Tell me what is in your heart. I want to listen; I want to understand. Tell me about your suffering and your difficulties. If you don't help me understand, who will?"

These are just examples. It's important that the words be your own. When you have the energy of compassion in your heart, your own loving words will come to you naturally. When you are very angry at someone, in the heat of the moment, it's almost impossible to use loving speech. But when understanding arises, compassion comes, and it's possible to use loving speech without having to make a lot of effort. A doctor who doesn't see the nature of the sickness can't help the patient. A psychotherapist who doesn't understand a patient's suffering can't help. Loving speech can open the door. Then you have an opportunity to practice deep listening and help the other person heal the relationship.

It takes courage to acknowledge difficulty in a relationship. You may think you will just wait until the other person comes to you first, but that may not happen. You can't wait. You can begin the practice of restoring communication by modeling open-hearted, compassionate dialogue. You may have to give yourself a deadline for making a start. When people come to weeklong retreats, I give them a deadline of the last night of the retreat to begin the reconciliation. If you are truly practicing, others will see that and be affected by it. They may not be able to show it right away, but what you say and the look in your eyes will have an effect.

The Suffering of Pride

There is a well-known Vietnamese story about a young couple who suffered deeply because they didn't practice mindful communication. The husband went off to war and left his pregnant wife behind. Three years later, when he was released from the army, his wife came to the village gate to welcome him and brought along their little boy. It was the first time the man had seen his child. When the young couple saw each other, they could not hold back the tears of joy. They were so grateful that the young man had survived and come home.

In Vietnam, there is a tradition that when an important event happens we make an offering on an altar to our ancestors and tell them what has happened. The wife went to the market to buy flowers, fruits, and other provisions for an offering to place on the altar. The father stayed home with his son and tried to persuade the little boy to call him "Daddy." But the little boy refused.

He said, "Mister, you aren't my daddy. My daddy is someone else. He used to come and visit us every night. Whenever he came, my mother would talk to him for a long time and cry and cry. When my mother sat down, the man sat down. When my mother lay down, he also lay down. So you are not my daddy." Hearing these words, the young father's heart turned to stone. He could no longer smile. He became silent.

When his wife returned, the man didn't look at her or speak to her anymore. He was very cold; he acted as though he despised her. She didn't understand why and she began to suffer deeply.

After the ceremony to make an offering to the ancestors, it's traditional to take the offering from the altar, and then the family sits down and enjoys the meal with happiness. But after the young man performed the offering, he didn't do this. He left the house, went into the village, and spent his time in the liquor shop. He got drunk because he couldn't bear his suffering. When the husband came home it was very late. He did the same thing every evening. He never talked to his wife, never looked at her, never ate at home. The young lady suffered so much she couldn't bear it, and on the fourth day she jumped into the river and drowned.

The evening after the funeral, the young father and the boy came home. As the man lit the kerosene lamp, the little boy shouted: "Here is my father!" and pointed to the shadow of his father on the wall. It turned out that the young woman used to talk to her shadow every night, because she missed her husband so much. One day the little boy had said, "Everyone in the village has a father, why don't I have one?" In order to calm the little boy, she pointed to her shadow that night on the wall, and said, "There is your father!" Of course when she sat down, the shadow would sit down too. Now the young father understood. His wrong perception had been wiped away. But it was too late.

What if the young man had gone to his wife and asked: "Darling, I've suffered so much the last few days. I don't think I can survive. Please help me. Please tell me who is that person who used to come every night, and with whom you talked and cried." That's a very simple thing to do. If he had done this, the young lady would have had a chance to explain, the tragedy would have been averted, and they would have recovered their happiness very easily. That's the direct way. But he didn't do this because he was so deeply hurt and his pride prevented him from going to her and asking for help.

The woman suffered so much as well. She was deeply hurt because of her husband's behavior, but she didn't ask for his help. Perhaps, if she'd asked her husband what was wrong, he would have told her what their son had said. But she didn't because she, too, was caught in pride.

A wrong perception can be the cause of a lot of suffering. All of us are subject to misunderstanding. We live with wrong perceptions every day. That's why we have to practice meditation and looking deeply into the nature of our perceptions. Whatever we perceive, we have to ask ourselves, "Are you sure your perception is right?" To be safe, you have to ask.

We're subject to many wrong perceptions in our daily lives. It may be that the other person didn't have the intention to hurt you. Mindful communication has the potential to ease so much of the unnecessary suffering in our relationships.

Reconciling in Families

Sometimes communication is hardest in our own family because families share similar suffering and ways of responding to suffering. The suffering of your parents was passed down from their parents and from their ancestors before them. Unless you begin to understand your own suffering and reconcile with yourself, that suffering will continue to be passed down to future generations. So we do the work of mindful communication not just for ourselves and our loved ones, but for our descendants.

Understanding your own suffering, you understand the suffering of your father. Your father may have had a lot of suffering and been unable to handle and transform the suffering, so he transmitted the whole mass of suffering to you. You inherit this suffering from him and from your mother.

When we're still young, many of us are determined to be different from our parents. We say we'll never make our children suffer. But when we grow up we tend to behave just like our parents, and we make others suffer because, like our ancestors, we don't know how to handle the energies we've inherited. We've received many positive and negative seeds from our parents and ancestors. They transmitted their habit to us because they didn't know how to transform it. Sometimes these habit energies have passed through many generations.

You have to recognize that you are the continuation of your father, mother, and ancestors. Cultivate mindfulness so you can recognize the habit energy each time it arises and embrace it with your energy of mindfulness. Each time we're able to do this, the habit energy becomes weaker. If we keep practicing like this, we can stop the cycle of transmission, and this will benefit not only us but our children and descendants. We can also help our children learn how to handle their habit energies and nourish the positive elements they have inside.

The suffering we received from our parents when we were children is probably our deepest suffering. We may hate our parents and feel that, whether or not they are still living, we will never reconcile with them. Yet with our practice of breathing mindfully, walking mindfully, and looking deeply, we can bring about transformation and restore communication in even the most difficult families. If the other person also practices mindful awareness, it's much easier, but reconciliation is possible even if the other person doesn't know about the practice.

Relationships with parents and siblings can be particularly difficult. Maybe during their childhood they were deeply wounded, and no one listened to them. So now they are perpetuating the cycle, and they don't want to listen to anyone. Don't ask your family members to change. When you're able to generate the energy of understanding and compassion in yourself, reconciliation can begin to take place.

I still remember a retreat in Oldenburg, in northern Germany. On the fourth day of the retreat, I gave everyone a midnight deadline to begin reconciling with someone with whom they had great difficulty. The next morning, one man came to me and said, "I've been so angry at my father for years. I couldn't even look at him. Even when I dialed his number last night, I doubted I could talk to him calmly." But when he heard his father's voice, he found that he naturally used loving speech; he didn't even have to try.

He said, "I know you've suffered a lot during the past many years. I'm sorry. I know I've acted and spoken in a way that didn't help. I didn't mean to make you suffer." His father heard the compassion in his son's voice and told him for the first time about his suffering and his difficulties.

Reconciliation is possible. You can find resolution to the difficulties in your relationships. You don't need to allow the difficulties to continue causing you to suffer month after month and year after year.

The first step is to practice mindful breathing, mindful walking, and mindfulness in daily activities, so that you will be strong enough to go back to yourself, listen to your own suffering, and look deeply into its nature. Unless we listen to our own suffering, there's no chance of improving the quality of our relationships. With mindfulness, compassion arises, and you can accept yourself. Then you have the chance to look at others. Even if they are not there with you, you can sit still and close your eyes and see the suffering they have gone through for so many years. When you can see the suffering in others, you begin to understand that there is a reason they suffer like that. You are no longer angry with them anymore. Compassion will arise in your heart. When compassion is born, you are more peaceful, your mind is clearer, and you will be motivated to say or do something to help others transform their difficulties. Reconciliation becomes possible.

Communicating in Long-Term Relationships

In long-term relationships, as in families, we often get in the habit of thinking that change isn't possible. We think the other person should change and they won't, so we give up hope. But we need to stop judging and return to our own internal communication. If we wait for our parents or our partner to change, it may take a very long time. If we wait for the other person to change, we may spend all our time waiting. So it's better that you change yourself. Don't try to force the other person to change. Even if it takes a long time, you will feel better when you are master of yourself and you are doing your best.

Sometimes when you see your partner behaving in a way that irritates you, you might want to reproach him or her. If you immediately try to correct him, he may get irritated, and then you both are irritated and become unkind. It is as if the blue sky disappears, the green trees disappear, and you are two blocks of suffering bumping against each other. This is the escalation of war, the escalation of unhappiness. You have to disentangle yourself from the unhappiness and go back to yourself, back to your peace, until you know how to handle the situation in a loving way.

Then, only when you are calm, invite your partner to speak. You can say you are sorry for not having understood her or him better. Only say this when you are ready. Then listen to her deeply, even if what she says is complaining, reproachful, or not very kind. You may learn that your partner has many wrong perceptions about you and about the situation, but try not to interrupt. Let her speak. Let her have a chance to speak out everything in her so she can feel listened to and understood. As your partner speaks, continue to breathe mindfully. Later on you may find a way to undo her misunderstanding, little by little in a very skillful, loving way, and mutual understanding will grow.

If your partner says something untrue, don't interrupt and say, "No, no, you're wrong. That wasn't my intention." Let him speak out. He's just trying to speak out the difficulty. If you interrupt, he will lose his inspiration to speak, and he will not tell you everything. You have plenty of time. You may even take a number of days to look deeply, in order to skillfully tell him about his wrong perception when he can hear it. You may have been angry with each other for years, and maybe because of just one condition, you're stuck and can't change the situation. If you can understand him deeply, you can start to make peace. Loving, compassionate speech and deep listening are the most powerful instruments for restoring communication. If you can understand and transform yourself, then you can help your partner.

Sometimes we're in a negative environment that doesn't leave us space to communicate with ourselves. Sometimes we may need to change the environment around us. But sometimes, in a relationship, we think separation or divorce is the only alternative. This is true if we're in a violent or abusive situation. It's important that we be in a place where we feel safe and not vulnerable. But if you are in a relationship where both people love each other and don't intentionally hurt each other, but you just don't know how to communicate, there may be other solutions. Many people think divorce is the solution, but after the papers are signed, they continue to suffer. If there are children or financial or other matters connecting you, you will still have to deal with each other for years to come. You can't take the other person out of you. You can't take yourself out of others. The suffering still continues. So the question is not whether you will stay together or not; the question is whether you can focus on trying to understand each other using compassionate speech and deep listening, no matter what the outcome.

Mutual Understanding in Challenging Situations

Compassionate communication is an extraordinarily powerful way to create mutual understanding and make changes. It can be used in situations where many people thought connection and communication impossible. It can transform situations where both parties are full of both fear and anger.

I have seen this when we've hosted groups of Israelis

and Palestinians at Plum Village. The first few days of such a retreat are always very difficult. In the beginning, both groups are full of fear, anger, and mistrust. The two groups don't even like to look at each other, they're so suspicious. They don't feel good when they look at each other because they've suffered a lot, and they believe that their suffering has been brought by the other side. During that first week, we focus solely on communicating with ourselves. Both groups practice and train in mindful breathing, nonthinking, and deep listening to themselves.

Only in the second week do we encourage the compassionate communication practices of deep listening and loving speech with each other. The group that speaks is encouraged to use the kind of language that could help the others understand the suffering they've gone through, the children as well as the adults. Each group tells the other about every kind of suffering they have undergone. But they do it using loving speech and trying not to blame or accuse.

We advise the listening group to listen with compassion. If they hear a misperception, they shouldn't try to interrupt and correct, because they will have plenty of time later on to help the other group correct their perceptions. When one group listens deeply to the other group, they recognize, maybe for the first time, that the other side has suffered very much, and that the suffering of the other group is very much like their own suffering, even if the circumstances are different. For many it's the first time that they recognize people on the other side as human beings just like them, who have suffered just like them.

When you understand their suffering, you feel compassion for them, and suddenly you don't hate anymore, you're not afraid of them anymore. Your way of looking at them has changed. They see compassion and acceptance in your eyes, and right away they suffer less.

These sessions of deep listening are organized in such a way that people have enough time to listen and talk about their suffering. Some of us who were present at these sessions were neither Palestinian nor Israeli. We were monks, nuns, and lay practitioners who came to sit and breathe with them and support their practice. We practiced mindful breathing and offered the collective energy of peace and mindfulness so they could practice listening with compassion. Our presence with the two groups was very important. We created a collective energy that supported mindful speech.

I think we can organize the same practice for ourselves or for any two groups who are divided. Sometimes Hindus are afraid of Muslims, and at the same time Muslims are afraid of Hindus. In other situations, Muslims are afraid of Christians and Christians are afraid of Muslims. We think of the other group as a threat to our survival and to our identity.

The first thing is to look deeply and see that not only on your side but also on the other side there's a lot of fear and suffering. In the beginning we think that we are the only ones who suffer and have a lot of fear. But if we get close enough to the other side and look, we see that they also have a lot of fear—fear of us—and also suffering. When we can see their suffering and fear, we suffer less already. When we're able to produce a compassionate thought, this thought begins to heal us, heal the other, and heal the world.

Peace Negotiations

I think if government officials organized peace talks the way we organize sessions of deep listening and loving speech, they would have more success in bringing reconciliation to opposing parties. When opposing parties come together to negotiate, they shouldn't negotiate right away. Each group has a lot of doubt, anger, and fear in them, and negotiating may be too challenging when these strong emotions are present. The first part of any peace initiative should be devoted to the practice of breathing, walking, sitting, and calming. Then the groups may be ready to listen to each other, and the desire and capacity for mutual understanding will be there to serve as a basis for successful negotiations.

If the atmosphere gets too heated during the negotiating session and the tension too strong, the chairperson should invite everyone to stop and breathe in and out to calm themselves down. Even if someone was in the middle of addressing the group, everyone should stop and breathe in and out together.

When I addressed a meeting of congressional representatives in Washington, D.C., I proposed a similar process. After that, we offered a retreat for a number of representatives, and we practiced mindfulness together. That was many years ago, but there are a few members of Congress who still practice mindful walking on Capitol Hill. It's possible and very beneficial to bring compassionate communication and mindful speech into political life.

There's no place where deep listening and loving speech are inappropriate. We don't need to save these techniques for a special occasion. They can be adapted to any situation and be helpful. If we use them now, we will have the understanding and insight we need to repair the damage we caused in the past and bring healing to ourselves, our families, our relationships, and our communities.

6

Mindful Communication
at Work

Successful work communication begins before we even arrive at our jobs. Often on our way to work—as we drive, bike, take the train, ride the bus, or walk—we focus on what we'll have to do when we arrive or on something we didn't finish before we left home.

If we instead bring our awareness to mindful breathing and to what's happening right in that moment, we can enjoy every moment of transporting ourselves to work. Before I begin my work of teaching for the day, I don't spend time worrying about what questions people might ask or how I might answer them. Instead, as I walk from my room to the place where I teach, I enjoy every step and every breath fully, and I live each moment of my walk deeply. This way, when I arrive, I feel fresh and ready to work. I can offer my best answer to any question I may be asked.

If you arrive at your workplace having already practiced mindfulness while getting ready at home and while on your way, you'll arrive happier and more relaxed than you have in the past, and successful communication will come a lot more easily.

The way you think about your work and your work relationships affects how you communicate in your work environment. You may be under the impression that the purpose of your work is to offer a service to others or to produce an object or commodity. But while at work, you're also producing thoughts, speech, and actions. Communication is as much a part of your job as is the end product. If you communicate well in your work environment, not only do you enjoy yourself more, but you create a harmonious atmosphere that will carry over into your work. Everything you do will have a stronger element of compassion and be of greater benefit to more people.

Leading by Example

When I was in India a number of years ago, I met Mr. K. R. Narayanan when he was the president of the Indian Parliament. We spoke about using the practice of deep listening and compassionate dialogue in legislative bodies. I said that any work environment, including a legislative assembly, could become a community motivated by mutual understanding and compassion. If we create a healthy and nourishing work community, we are modeling the kind of environment we want to create in the world.

When, in a work environment, you use mindful and compassionate speech, you're offering the best of yourself. If we can combine our insights and experiences the collective insight will bring about the wisest decisions. If we're not able to listen to our colleagues with a free heart, if we only consider and support ideas that we already know and agree with, we're harming our work environment. Whatever your position is at work, you can set an example by learning to listen to everyone with equal interest and concern.

Many workplaces are characterized by daily stress. We need to set up spaces at work for the practice of mindful breathing. Mindful breathing is the first step to mindful communicating because it relaxes us in body and mind. We have to be relaxed, to feel well, so that we can make the best decisions possible. When we model relaxation at work, we are already communicating powerfully.

Mr. Narayanan and I talked about integrating mindful breathing into the Parliament of India as a way to reduce stress. If they can do it in the legislature, perhaps you can do it in your workplace. Can you bring your colleagues together to practice mindful breathing or make time available for this before any group meeting so that people will be able to communicate more effectively and without stress? If you can't organize others, even your own mindful breathing will make your work communication go better. Sometimes workplace communication can seem so difficult, but one mindful breath already begins to make it easier.

Greeting Your Colleagues

What is the first thing you do when you arrive at work? Do you smile at the people you see? Do you greet them? The first few minutes are crucial in setting the tone for your workday. You may feel you have too much on your mind. You may still be absorbed in an argument or in something challenging that happened before you arrived. But if you've spent the time getting to work breathing mindfully and being in the present moment, you will arrive with a clear mind and you'll be able to greet people with a warm and open smile. This is part of your job, no matter what your profession.

Answering the Phone

At work, many of us communicate not just with the people around us but by e-mail, telephone, or video conferencing. Some of us work primarily with people who aren't in the same physical space or even in the same time zone or country. Even so, you can turn every phone conversation or e-mail into an opportunity to practice compassionate communication. Whenever the phone rings, you can hear it as a bell of mindfulness and stop whatever you're doing. Instead of rushing to answer the phone, you can breathe in and out with awareness three times before answering to make sure you're truly present for whoever is calling. Recognize any feelings of stress or irritation you may have or any feeling that you're being interrupted. You may want to put your hand on the receiver while breathing to let your coworkers know that you intend to pick up the phone, but you're just not in a hurry. This will help remind them that they don't need to feel like they're victims of the telephone.

You can use the same practice before reading an e-mail. At work we often go from one e-mail to the next without first practicing mindful breathing and making ourselves present for whatever that e-mail has to say. If we wait until we've taken a few mindful breaths and returned to being fully present before we open an e-mail, it's true that it will take us a little longer to go through our mail, and our work might be a bit slower. But our communication with each e-mail will be more effective, clearer, and more understanding.

If you want to send an e-mail or call someone on the phone, you might want to recite the following verse to yourself before you begin to type or to dial the number:

Words can travel thousands of miles.
May my words create mutual understanding and love.
May they be as beautiful as gems,
as lovely as flowers.

Mindful Meetings

Our communication in meetings can often be a source of tension, stress, and conflict at work. Sometimes we rush from one meeting to another, so we arrive already anxious or distracted.

It will help to schedule a few minutes at the beginning of any meeting to sit quietly together. If people in your workplace are open to having a bell sound before the meeting begins, that sound can help everyone come back to their breathing and find some calm. If people don't want to start the meeting by sitting together quietly for a few moments, you can still arrive at the meeting a few minutes early so you have time to relax and breathe mindfully. Perhaps other people will see your example and join you the next time. You don't need to say anything or make a point of letting others know you're doing this. Just do it and enjoy the benefit it brings you.

It can be helpful in setting the tone of a meeting to open with a spoken agreement that the participants will respect each other's words and be open to the views of others. If we try to impose our views on others, we only create tension and suffering at work. So in any meeting, practice being open and listening to the experience and insight of others.

If you have a wonderful idea and are eager to share it, that's good, but you shouldn't be so eager to share your ideas that you drown out the ideas of others. Invite everybody to express their ideas. Trust that the best ideas will emerge from this process as collective wisdom.

During the meeting, practice using loving speech and deep listening. Follow your breathing as you listen. Let one person speak at a time, without interruption. Don't get caught up in verbal duels. Speak from your own experience, and address the whole group whenever you talk. If you have questions or concerns, place them in the center of the circle for the whole group to contemplate and address. This may be challenging; it is likely a new culture for conducting meetings, one that is different from the way meetings have been run in the past. You don't have to try to change the culture all at once. If everyone agrees to listen mindfully and without interruption, that is wonderful. But even if it's only you who follows these guidelines and makes a commitment to speak and listen with compassion, it will have a positive effect.

Creating Community at Work

If you're modeling compassionate communication at work, soon others may be interested in practicing mindful breathing, sitting, and walking with you. If you're surrounded by people who are practicing mindfulness together, you'll all be supported by the collective energy, and mindful speech and deep listening will come much more easily.

The more you practice mindfulness, the more you'll see things you can do to change your work environment in a positive way. When we practice mindful speech and deep listening, our way of communicating becomes a bell of mindfulness for everyone. When you walk mindfully, enjoying every step you take, this encourages others to do the same, even if they don't know that you're practicing mindfulness. When you smile, your smile supports everyone around you and also reminds others to smile. When you practice, your presence has a positive effect on you and those around you.

A Rock in the River

All of us have difficulties at work sometimes. We all have our own pain, sorrows, and fears. Often at work we don't give ourselves time or space to recognize and embrace these strong emotions, so our tension comes out in unintentional ways. This can make communication difficult.

But none of us needs to embrace pain and sorrow alone. When you throw a rock into a river, no matter how small the rock is, it will sink to the bottom of the river. But if you have a boat, you can carry many tons of rocks, and they won't sink. The same is true of our suffering. Our sorrow, fear, worries, and pain are like rocks that can be carried by the boat of mindfulness. If we give ourselves the time and space to embrace and recognize the suffering, we won't sink into the ocean of anger, worries, or sorrow. We become lighter.

We can practice mindfulness alone, but we can find more ease and joy if we can bring mindful communication into our work environments and have the support of others who are practicing mindfulness with us. Don't expect to change your work environment overnight. But if you make a diligent effort to practice compassionate communication, both with yourself and with your colleagues, you're taking steps in the right direction, and that is good enough.

7

Creating Community
in the World

As powerful as compassionate communication can be when we use it in our individual relationships, its power is magnified when we bring it to our communities. Both *communication* and *community* have the same Latin root, *communicare,* meaning to impart, share, or make common. We need to go in the direction of reconciliation and understanding, not just with our friends and family, but in our neighborhoods and workplaces. We can create an inclusive, compassionate foundation as the basis from which we interact with everyone.

A community that is committed to mindful speech and deep listening can be very effective in making society better. These two practices could be part of a global ethic that would be available to people of any culture or religious tradition to reduce conflict and restore communication.

Community Creates Change

We can speak of our practice in terms of energy because mindfulness is a kind of energy. When we bring our energies together, they are increased a thousandfold. The whole can be much, much greater than the sum of its parts. Systematic change can't be achieved without the energy of community. If you want to save the planet, if you want to transform society, you need a strong community. Technology is not enough. Without mindfulness, technology can be more destructive than constructive. When we speak about creating a sustainable environment or a more just society, we usually speak of physical action or technological advances as the means to achieve these goals. But we forget about the element of a connected community. Without that, we can't do anything at all.

Usually we think of communal action in terms of physical acts, but the energy of a shared meditative silence or communal chanting is also communication and a powerful kind of action. I don't think of this concentration so much as prayer or a religious rite, but rather as a form of communication. When we sit and concentrate as a community, we create a collective energy that has compassion and awakened understanding in it. Sitting together in silence can be a practice of listening to our own suffering and the suffering of the world.

The collective energy of mindfulness also supports our individual practice. When we see other people who are in good communication with themselves and others, they inspire us. Sometimes the cause of our sorrow is hidden by so many layers of suffering that we can't penetrate it by ourselves, even when we practice diligently and sit mindfully. In these cases, the energy of a community of mindfulness can help us embrace and release suffering that we could not reach by ourselves. If we open our hearts, the collective energy of the community can penetrate the suffering inside us. Mindful listening and speaking will make it easier for us to build a stronger community.

Building Trust and Sharing Suffering

Some of us do not easily trust another person. For such a person, it can be difficult to imagine sharing with a larger community. We may be a little bit wary or even very suspicious. People say they love us and understand us, but we haven't really experienced that love and understanding. We should be able to find ways to help a person who doesn't have the capacity to receive love and understanding. Sometimes there is real love, there is real understanding, but the person doesn't believe in love and understanding, and that's why he has never been able to receive it. That person is like a hungry ghost. In Buddhism, a "hungry ghost" is someone who has a big, empty stomach and is very hungry but has a very tiny throat. Even if there's plenty of food, that person can't swallow it. He can't absorb anything. So even if a lot of understanding and love is offered, that person isn't able to take it in.

A person who suffers like that has no capacity to receive understanding, love, and help. You have to be very patient. From time to time we see hungry ghosts like that walking around, and we can recognize them easily. They look very alone and cut off. We have to be very patient and allow them a lot of time and space. Don't be too eager to help, because when you're too eager to help, you may have the opposite effect from what you intended, and you may get an opposite response.

Remain fresh, loving, compassionate, and spacious for them. That is what you can do now. Look deeply to see if you can find a mantra to say that's skillful enough to help them enlarge their throats and get nourishment. With patience and time, one day their throats will be larger, and they will begin to notice the energy of love and understanding that is in you. Community building takes time.

Community Strengthens Compassion

Scientists have studied the behavior of social animals, such as birds and fish, and have found that in every community there is an element of altruism; some members of the community are ready to die and sacrifice their lives for the sake of the community.

There is a kind of fish called a stickleback. They swim in bands, thousands of them. Whenever they notice the shadow of a predator, a large fish that might threaten the band of fish, a few dozen will detach themselves and go explore. They know there's a risk, but they want to go in that direction to see if the threat is real. If they find there's no risk, they go back and rejoin the band of fish. If there is a real danger, a few of them will stay to be swallowed by the big fish while the rest go back and tell the band of fish to go in another direction. Ants also behave like that, as do bees and some kinds of birds. We humans also hear news reports of heroes sacrificing themselves in this way.

This behavior on the part of some members of your community nourishes your own generosity and altruism.

Scientists in this fish study found that if a school stays together, the generosity will grow. The descendants will profit and become more and more generous. But if they are dispersed, the generosity dies down very quickly.

According to scientists who have conducted studies, when you're exposed to such behavior from some members of your community, the seed of altruism in you is watered. And when your turn comes, you will do the same—you will know how to sacrifice for the sake of the community.

Living in the world, we have strong habits. We walk without any awareness or enjoyment of our steps. We walk as if we have to run. We speak but don't know what we are saying; we create a lot of suffering while speaking. Communities that commit themselves to mindfulness can help members of the community learn how to speak, breathe, and walk mindfully. The community helps train you, and you train yourself.

When we practice in a community, there are more people to support us but also more opportunities for frustration and anger. Loving speech and deep listening are key to community building. You learn to speak in a way that will not cause suffering in yourself and your community. If your community doesn't practice this, it's not an authentic community. Even if you have suffering and anger, you can train yourself to speak in a way that helps the other person or group understand what is going on in you, and that makes real communication possible.

Our World Can Be a Mindful, Compassionate Community

We need to find better ways to communicate. If we can do this in our relationships, we can do it in our work environments, and even in our political environments. We have to transform our governments into mindful, compassionate places of deep listening and loving speech. We each can do our part to contribute as a citizen, as a member of the human family. In the process of community building we get the transformation and healing we need to further the transformation and healing of the world.

This is a process of training and learning. When you speak, allow the insight of our collective humanity to speak through you. When you walk, don't walk for yourself alone; walk for your ancestors and your community. When you breathe, allow the larger world to breathe for you. When you're angry, allow your anger to be released and to be embraced by the larger community. If you know how to do this for one day, you are already transformed. Be your community and let your community be you. This is true practice. Be like the river when it arrives at the ocean; be like the bees and birds that fly together. See yourself in the community and see the community in you. This is a process of transforming your way of seeing, and it will transform how, and how effectively, you communicate.

8

Our Communication Is Our Continuation

Every human and every animal communicates. We typically think of communication as the words we use when we speak or write, but our body language, our facial expressions, our tone of voice, our physical actions, and even our thoughts are ways of communicating.

Just as an orange tree can produce beautiful orange leaves, blossoms, and fruits, a beautiful human being can produce beautiful thoughts, speech, and actions. Our communication is not neutral. Every time we communicate, we either produce more compassion, love, and harmony or we produce more suffering and violence.

Our communication is what we put out into the world and what remains after we have left it. In this way, our communication is our karma. The Sanskrit word *karma* means "action," and it refers not just to bodily action but to what we express with our bodies, our words, and our thoughts and intentions.

Throughout our day, we produce energies of thought, speech, and action. We're communicating in every moment, either with ourselves or with others. Thinking, speech, and bodily acts are our own manifestations. You *are* your action. You are what you do, not only what you do with your body, but also with your words and your mind. Karma is the triple action of our thoughts, our speech, and our bodily actions.

Thinking is already action. Even if you don't see its manifestation, it is there as powerful energy. Thinking can push you to do or say things that are destructive, or it can create a lot of love. Every thought will bring a fruit, sometimes right away, sometimes later on. When you produce a thought of hate, anger, or despair, that thought is a poison which will affect your body and your mind. A thought of hatred or anger can lead one person to hurt another. If you commit a violent act, it means you've been producing thoughts of hatred, anger, and the desire to punish. So thinking is already acting. You don't need to say or do anything in order to be acting. To produce a thought is to act.

When you produce a thought that is full of under-standing, forgiveness, and compassion, that thought will immediately have a healing effect on both your physical and mental health and on those around you. If you think a thought that is full of judgment and anger, that thought will immediately poison your body and mind and the people around you.

Thinking is the first kind of action, because our thinking is the basis for how we affect the world. Our speaking also has a huge effect. If we're capable of speaking and writing with compassion and understanding, we feel wonderful in our bodies and in our minds. We don't speak with compassion just so that the person or people we're speaking to will feel better! Our compassionate speech has a healing effect on us too. After you have been able to say something kind, forgiving, and compassionate, you feel much better.

When you write words full of compassion and forgiveness, you feel freer, even if the person you're writing to hasn't read them yet. Even before you mail the letter or send the e-mail or text, you feel better. The person reading your words will also feel your compassion. In the same way, if you speak with anger and violence, if you speak out of a desire to punish, both you and the people who hear your words experience more suffering. Think of a child hearing her parents fighting. Even if the words are not directed at her, the effect of the angry speech is much the same. Speech, the second form of action, can heal and liberate, or it can cause destruction and pain.

The third form of action is bodily action. We communicate with our body language (our clenched fists or open arms), but also with our larger actions (including what we choose to show up for, what we do with our day, and how we treat others). If you are able to do something in the line of saving, supporting, protecting, comforting, rescuing, or caring, there is a positive effect right away.

Every Communication Bears Our Signature

Everything we say and do bears our signature. We can't say, "That's not my thought." We're responsible for our own communication. So if it happens that yesterday I said something that wasn't right, I have to do something today to transform it. The French philosopher Jean-Paul Sartre said, "Man is the sum of all his actions." The value of our lives depends on the quality of our thinking, our speech, and our action.

We want to offer the best kind of thinking, the best kind of speech, and the best kind of bodily acts, because those actions are our continuation. When we think, when we speak, when we act, we create, and we are there in our creations. That is the outcome of our being. Our communications will not be lost when our physical bodies are no longer here. The effect of our thinking, speech, and physical actions will continue to ripple outward into the cosmos. Whether this body is still here or has disintegrated, our actions continue.

When you produce a thought, it bears your signature. It's *you* who produced that thought, and you are responsible for it. If it's a thought of compassion, forgiveness, non-discrimination, you will continue beautifully, because you are there in it. You are the author of that action. Your speech and your physical actions, both compassionate and violent, also bear your signature.

We are like the cloud that produces the rain. Through the rain, the cloud continues to affect the crops, the trees, and the rivers, even after the cloud is no longer floating there in the sky. Likewise, everything we produce in terms of thought, speech, and action continues even after our bodies disintegrate. The cloud is there in the cornfield and in the river. When this body disintegrates, our words, thoughts, and physical actions continue to have an effect. Our thoughts, speech, and actions are our real continuation.

According to this practice, it's possible to continue beautifully into the future. Imagine a bank account somewhere in which we deposit every word, thought, and physical action. The bank account certainly does exist, but its nature is nonlocal. Nothing is lost.

Changing the Past

Suppose in the past you said something unkind to your grandmother. Now she is no longer alive, so you can't apologize directly to her. Many of us carry the guilt of something we have said or done that we think we can't rectify. But it's possible to erase that unskillfulness of the past. The past isn't exactly gone. If we know our communication continues, then we know the past is still there, disguised in the present moment. After all, the suffering is still there; you can touch it.

What you can do is to sit down, breathe in and out deeply, and recognize that in every cell of your body there is the presence of your grandmother. "Grandma, I know that you are there in every cell of my body; I am your continuation. I'm sorry I said something that made you suffer and made me suffer. Please listen, Grandma. I promise that from now on, I won't say such a thing to anyone anymore. Grandma, please accept helping me in this practice." When you talk to your grandmother like that, you can see her smiling to you, and you heal the suffering of the past.

Communication isn't static. Even if yesterday you produced a thought of anger and hate, today you can produce a thought in the opposite direction, a thought of compassion and tolerance. As soon as we produce the new thought, it can very quickly catch up with yesterday's thought and neutralize it. Using right communication today can help us heal the past, enjoy the present, and prepare the ground for a good future.

9

Practices for Compassionate Communication

The Computer Bell

Many times when we work with our computers, we are completely lost in our work, and we forget to be in touch with ourselves. Or we may forget to pay attention to our conversations, getting carried away in juicy gossip, criticizing, complaining, or other unmindful speech.

We can program a bell of mindfulness on our computers, and every quarter of an hour (or as often as we like), the bell sounds and we have a chance to stop and go back to ourselves. Breathing in and out three times is enough to release the tension in the body and smile, and then we can continue our work.

Drinking Tea in Mindfulness

Drinking tea is a wonderful way to set aside time to communicate with yourself. When I drink my tea, I just

drink my tea. I don't have to think. I can stop all my
thinking while I drink my tea. When I stop my thinking,
I can focus my attention on the tea. There is only the
tea. There is only me. Between me and the tea there is a
connection. I don't need a telephone to talk to the tea. In
fact, because I'm not on the telephone, I can get more in
touch with the tea. I just breathe in, and I'm aware that my
in-breath is there, I'm aware that my body is there, and I'm
aware that the tea is there.

It's wonderful to make the time to just drink your tea.
In Zen Buddhism we don't normally use commandments
as hard and fast rules, but "Drink your tea!" is like a Zen
commandment to bring you back to your true home. Don't
think. Be there, body and mind united. Establish yourself
in the here and the now. You are true. You are not a
phantom; you are real, and you know what is going on.
What is going on is that there is a cup of tea in your hands.

Listening to Your Inner Child

Every one of us has a wounded child within who needs
our care and love. But we run away from our inner child
because we're afraid of the suffering. In addition to
listening to others with compassion, we must also listen
to the wounded child inside us. That little child needs our

attention. Take time to go back and tenderly embrace the wounded child within you. You can talk to the child with the language of love. "Dear one, in the past, I left you alone. I've gone away from you for so long. I'm sorry. Now I have come back to take care of you, to embrace you. I know you suffer so much, and I have neglected you. But now I've learned the way to take care of you. I am here now." If we have to, we can cry with that child. Whenever we sit, we can spend time sitting and breathing with that child. "Breathing in, I go back to my wounded child; breathing out, I take good care of my wounded child." When we go for a walk, we can take the hand of our little child.

We should talk to our child several times a day for healing to take place. The little child has been left alone for a long time, so we need to begin this practice right away. Go back to your inner child every day and listen for five or ten minutes, and healing will take place.

Our wounded child is not only us; he or she may represent several generations of ancestors. Our parents and ancestors may have suffered all their lives without knowing how to look after the wounded child in themselves, so they transmitted that child to us. So when we're embracing the wounded child inside us, we're embracing all the wounded children of past generations.

This practice doesn't just benefit us; it liberates numberless generations of ancestors and descendants. This practice can break the cycle.

Writing a Love Letter

If you have difficulties with someone in your life, you might spend some time alone and write that person a real letter. You can write the letter to someone you see every day or, just as effectively, to someone you haven't seen for years, or even to someone who is no longer living. It is never too late to bring peace and healing into a relationship. Even if we no longer see that person, we can reconcile inside ourselves, and the relationship can heal.

Give yourself a couple of hours to write a letter using loving speech. While you write the letter, practice looking deeply into the nature of your relationship. Why has communication been difficult? Why has happiness not been possible? Here is an example:

My dear,

I know you have suffered a lot over the past many years. I have not been able to help you—in fact, I have made the situation worse. It is not my intention to make you suffer. Maybe I'm not skillful enough. Maybe I tried to impose my ideas on you. In the past I thought you made me suffer. Now I realize that I have been responsible for my own suffering.

I promise to do my best to refrain from saying things or doing things that make you suffer. Please tell me what is in your heart. You need to help me; otherwise it is not possible for me to do it. I can't do it alone.

· You have nothing to risk by writing this letter. You can even decide later whether to send it. But whether you send it or not, you will find that the person who finishes writing the letter is not the same person who began it—peace, understanding, and compassion have transformed you.

Peace Treaties and Peace Notes

The peace treaty and the peace note are two tools to help us heal anger and hurt in our relationships. The peace treaty can be used as a preventive tool, before we utter or are hurt by words or actions that seem unkind. When we sign the peace treaty, we are making peace not just with the other person but within ourselves.

The peace note can be used as a healing tool when we're hurt or angry because of something someone has said or done. You can copy it and keep blank copies available wherever you need it. You can use it in place of the fourth mantra note that you keep in your wallet.

If someone does something that brings us suffering, we can say, "What you just said hurt me. I would like to look deeply into it, and I would like you to also look deeply into it. Let's make an appointment for sometime later in the week to look at it together." One person looking at the roots of our suffering is good, two people looking is better, and two people looking together is best.

Both the treaty and the note suggest waiting a few days for discussion. You can pick any night. First, you are still hurt, and it may be too risky if you begin discussing it now. You might say things that will make the situation worse. From now until that evening, you can practice looking deeply into the nature of your suffering, and the other person can too. Before that night, one or both of you may see the root of the problem and be able to tell the other and apologize. Then on that night, you can have a cup of tea together and enjoy each other.

If by that evening the suffering has not been transformed, one person begins by expressing himself, while the other person listens deeply. When you speak, you tell the deepest kind of truth using loving speech, the kind of speech the other person can understand and accept. While listening, you know that your listening must be of good quality to relieve the other person of his suffering. If you can, have the discussion be on a Friday evening or early on a Saturday, so you still have the weekend to enjoy being together.

Peace Treaty

In order that we may live long and happily together, in order that we may continually develop and deepen our love and understanding, we the undersigned vow to observe and practice the following:

I, the one who is angry, agree to:

1. Refrain from saying or doing anything that might cause further damage or escalate the anger.
2. Not suppress my anger.
3. Practice breathing and taking refuge in the island of myself.
4. Calmly, within twenty-four hours, tell the one who has made me angry about my anger and suffering, either verbally or by delivering a peace note.
5. Ask for an appointment for later in the week (e.g., Friday evening) to discuss this matter more thoroughly, either verbally or by peace note.

6. Not say, "I am not angry. It's okay. I am not suffering. There is nothing to be angry about, at least not enough to make me angry."

7. Practice breathing and looking deeply into my daily life—while sitting, lying down, standing, and walking—to see:

   a. the ways I myself have been unskillful at times.
   b. how I have hurt the other person because of my habit energy.
   c. how the strong seed of anger in me is the primary cause of my anger.
   d. how the other person's suffering, which waters the seed of my anger, is the secondary cause.
   e. how the other person is only seeking relief from his or her own suffering.
   f. that as long as the other person suffers, I cannot be truly happy.

8. Apologize immediately, without waiting until our appointment, as soon as I realize my unskillfulness and lack of mindfulness.

9. Postpone the meeting if I do not feel calm enough to meet with the other person.

I, the one who has made the other angry, agree to:

1. Respect the other person's feelings, not ridicule him or her, and allow enough time for him or her to calm down.
2. Not press for an immediate discussion.
3. Confirm the other person's request for a meeting, either verbally or by note, and assure him or her that I will be there.
4. Practice breathing and taking refuge in the island of myself to see how:

   a. I have seeds of unkindness and anger as well as habit energy to make the other person unhappy.
   b. I have mistakenly thought that making the other person suffer would relieve my own suffering.
   c. by making him or her suffer, I make myself suffer.

5. Apologize as soon as I realize my unskillfulness and lack of mindfulness, without making any attempt to justify myself and without waiting until the meeting.

We vow to abide by these articles and to practice wholeheartedly.

Signed,

the _____ day of _____

in the year _____ in _____.

Peace Note

Date:

Time:

Dear _____,

This morning/afternoon/yesterday, you said/did something that made me very angry. I suffered very much. I want you to know this. You said/did: _____

_____.

Please let us both look at what you said/did and examine the matter together in a calm and open manner this Friday evening.

Yours, not very happy right now,

_____

Beginning Anew

When a difficulty arises in our relationships and one of us feels resentment or hurt, a good practice to try is called "beginning anew." To begin anew is to look deeply and honestly at ourselves—our past actions, speech, and thoughts—and to create a fresh beginning within ourselves and in our relationships with others.

Beginning anew helps us develop our kind speech and compassionate listening because it is a practice of recognition and appreciation of the positive elements of another person. Recognizing others' positive traits allows us to also see our own good qualities. Along with these good traits, we each have areas of weakness, such as talking out of our anger or being caught in our misperceptions. As in a garden, when we "water the flowers" of loving kindness and compassion in each other, we also take energy away from the weeds of anger, jealousy, and misperception.

We can practice beginning anew every day by expressing our appreciation to the people we care about and apologizing right away when we do or say something that hurts them. We can also politely let others know when we have been hurt.

A more formal beginning anew can be done weekly in families and in work situations. It is a three-part process: watering flowers, expressing regrets, and expressing hurts and difficulties. This practice can prevent feelings of hurt from building up over weeks and helps make the situation safe for everyone in the workplace or family.

Flower watering is the first part of the practice. Flower watering is simply showing appreciation for the others in your family or work community. People do it one at a time, waiting until they feel moved to speak. The others let them speak without response. It is helpful for people to hold a vase of flowers or some object in front of them as they speak, so that their words reflect the freshness and beauty of the flowers. During flower watering, the speaker acknowledges the wholesome, wonderful qualities of the others. It is not flattery; we need to speak the truth. Everyone has strong points that can be seen with awareness. No one can interrupt the person holding the flowers. Each person is allowed as much time as needed, and everyone else practices deep listening. When one person has finished speaking, he or she stands up and slowly returns the vase to the center of the room.

We should not underestimate the first step of flower watering. When we sincerely recognize the beautiful qualities of other people, it is very difficult to hold on to our feelings of anger and resentment. We naturally soften, and our perspective becomes wider and more inclusive of the whole reality.

In the second part of the practice, participants express regret for anything they have done to hurt others. It does not take more than one thoughtless phrase to hurt someone. Sometimes we hold on to some small resentment or regret, and it grows because we don't have the time to make it right. The practice of beginning anew is an opportunity for us to recall some regret from earlier in the week and undo it.

In the third part of the ceremony, we express ways in which others have hurt us. Loving speech is crucial. We want to heal our families and work communities, not harm them. We speak frankly, but we don't want to be destructive. When we sit among people who are all practicing deep listening, our speech becomes more beautiful and more constructive. We never blame or argue.

In this final part of the practice, compassionate listening is crucial. We listen to another's hurts and difficulties with the willingness to relieve the suffering of the other person, not to judge or argue. We listen with all our attention. Even if we hear something that is not true, we continue to listen deeply so the other person can express his or her pain and release the tensions within. If we reply or correct that person, the practice will not bear fruit. We just listen. If we need to tell others that their perception was not correct, we can do that a few days later, privately and calmly. Then, at the next beginning anew practice, they may rectify the error themselves, and we will not have to say anything. We can end the practice with a moment of silence.

Just practicing the first part of beginning anew—flower watering—can increase the happiness and communication in your family or your workplace. You don't need to do all three parts each time. Especially when the practice is new to you, it will work to spend most of your time on flower watering. Then slowly over time, as trust is built, you can add the second and third parts. Even then, don't skip over the first. Expressing appreciation is one of the greatest ways of building strong and caring relationships.

The Cake in the Refrigerator

One tool we can use to improve our communication is a cake. It doesn't matter if you're not a baker, don't have a cake, or are gluten-free. This is a very special cake that is not made of flour and sugar like a sponge cake. We can keep eating it, and it is never finished. It is called "the cake in the refrigerator."

This practice was developed to help children deal with their parents' arguing, but it can also be used by adults in a relationship. When the atmosphere becomes heavy and unpleasant, and it seems that one person is losing his or her temper, you can use the practice of the cake to restore harmony.

First of all, breathe in and out three times to give yourself courage. Then turn to the person or people who seem upset and let them know you just remembered something. When they ask you what, you can say, "I remember that we have a cake in the refrigerator."

Saying, "there is a cake in the refrigerator" really means: "Please, let's not make each other suffer anymore." Hearing these words, the person will understand. Hopefully, he or she will look at you and say, "That's right. I'll go and get the cake." This is a nonjudgmental way out of a dangerous situation. The person who is upset now has an opportunity to withdraw from the fight without causing more tension.

The person goes into the kitchen, opens the refrigerator to take out the cake, and boils water to make the tea, all the while following their breathing. If there is no real cake in the refrigerator, something else can be substituted—a piece of fruit or toast or whatever you find. Preparing the snack and tea, that person may even remember to smile as a way to feel lighter in body and spirit.

While sitting alone in the living room, the other person can begin to practice breathing in mindfulness. Gradually hot tempers will calm down. After the tea and cake have been placed on the table, perhaps all will join the tea party in an atmosphere that is light and full of understanding. If one person is hesitant to take part, you can coax him or her by saying, "Please come and have some tea and cake with me."

Hugging Meditation

Some of our strongest communication does not include words. When we hug, our hearts connect and we know we are not separate beings. Hugging with mindfulness and concentration can bring reconciliation, healing, understanding, and much happiness.

You may practice hugging meditation with a friend, your daughter, your father, your partner, or even with a tree. To practice, first bow and recognize the presence of the other. Close your eyes, take a deep breath, and visualize yourself and your beloved three hundred years from now. Then you can enjoy three deep, conscious breaths to bring yourself fully there. You can say to yourself: "Breathing in, I know that life is precious in this moment. Breathing out, I cherish this moment of life."

Smile at the person in front of you, expressing your desire to hold her in your arms. This is a practice and a ritual. When you bring your body and mind together to produce your total presence, to become full of life, it is a ritual.

When I drink a glass of water, I invest one hundred percent of myself in drinking it. You should train yourself to live every moment of your daily life like that. Hugging is a deep practice. You need to be totally present to do it correctly.

Then open your arms and begin hugging. Hold each other for three in- and out-breaths. With the first breath, you are aware that you are present in this very moment, and you are happy. With the second breath, you are aware that the other is present in this moment, and she is also happy. With the third breath, you are aware that you are here together, right now on this earth, and you feel deep gratitude and happiness for your togetherness. You then may release the other person and bow to each other to show your thanks.

You can also practice it in the following way: During the first in-breath and out-breath, become aware that you and your beloved are both alive. For the second in-breath and out-breath, think of where you will both be three hundred years from now. And for the third in-breath and out-breath, go back to the insight that you are both alive.

When you hug in such a way, the other person becomes real and alive. You do not need to wait until one of you is ready to depart for a trip; you may hug right now and receive the warmth and stability of your friend in the present moment. Hugging can be a deep practice of reconciliation.

During the silent hugging, the message will come out clearly: "Darling, you are precious to me. I am sorry I have not been mindful and considerate. I have made mistakes. Allow me to begin anew."

Life becomes real at that moment. Architects need to build airports and railway stations so that there is enough room to practice hugging. Your hugging will be deeper, and so will your happiness.

Thich Nhat Hanh has retreat communities in southwestern France (Plum Village), New York (Blue Cliff Monastery), and California (Deer Park Monastery), where monks, nuns, laymen, and laywomen practice the art of mindful living. Visitors are invited to join the practice for at least one week. For information, please write to:

Plum Village
13 Martineau
33580 Dieulivol
France
NH-office@plumvillage.org (for women)
LH-office@plumvillage.org (for women)
UH-office@plumvillage.org (for men)
www.plumvillage.org

For information about our monasteries, mindfulness practice centers, and retreats in the United States, please contact:

Blue Cliff Monastery
3 Hotel Road
Pine Bush, NY 12566
Tel: (845) 733-4959
www.bluecliffmonastery.org

Deer Park Monastery
2499 Melru Lane
Escondido, CA 92026
Tel: (760) 291-1003
Fax: (760) 291-1172
www.deerparkmonastery.org
deerpark@plumvillage.org